Giving Academic Presentations

Second Edition

Giving Academic Presentations

Second Edition

Susan M. Reinhart

 MICHIGAN SERIES IN ENGLISH FOR
ACADEMIC & PROFESSIONAL PURPOSES

Ann Arbor
UNIVERSITY OF MICHIGAN PRESS

Copyright © by the University of Michigan 2002, 2013
All rights reserved
ISBN 978-0-472-03509-0
Published in the United States of America
The University of Michigan Press
Manufactured in the United States of America

∞ Printed on acid-free paper

ISBN 978-0-472-03509-0

2020   2019   2018   2017   8   7   6   5

To my nieces and nephew

Alex
Liz
Adrienne
Robin
Caroline
Kim
Ted

With love

Acknowledgments

Christine Feak helped me envision the first edition of the text, evaluated portions of the text, and contributed materials to it. John Swales provided extensive comments. Scott Baxter and his students at the School of English, Adam Mickiewicz University, Poznań, Poland, classroom tested the manuscript and provided valuable feedback. MICASE Project Manager Rita Simpson, Sarah Briggs, and the MICASE office staff supported my attempts to find appropriate scripts from MICASE. Judy Dyer offered feedback on materials she used in her class and Pamela Bogart provided Task 5 in Unit 3 of the first edition. Philomena Meechan at the Language Resource Center helped with technical advice. Roann Altman and Meg Rosse gave useful suggestions for improving the manuscript. Other colleagues at ELI, especially Carolyn Madden, supported me during the writing process. Anonymous reviewers gave me many suggestions for improving the text. My father, Fred Reinhart, provided me a welcoming, quiet place to visit, and Margo Czinski and Ann Sinsheimer gave me their friendship and encouragement.

Mindy Matice and Judy Dyer offered a number of suggestions for the second edition of the text. John Swales facilitated my escape from the isolation of textbook revising by giving me advice while we went birding. My students played a major role in developing both editions of the text. I am indebted to them for helping me rethink materials for this second edition. Finally, a special thank you to Melinda Slawson who provided extensive feedback. A number of her suggestions have been incorporated.

The University of Michigan Press acknowledges the students who have allowed their work to appear in both editions of *Giving Academic Presentations*.

Contents

Introduction to the Second Edition

Giving Academic Presentations is a speaking text specifically written to prepare university-level students to make presentations in an academic setting. To carry out this goal, the text addresses a range of skills and strategies that speakers of academic English need to become successful presenters. It provides information and hands-on tasks designed to enhance a speaker's performance and thereby maximize communication with members of the audience–faculty, fellow students, and colleagues.

Giving Academic Presentations was primarily written for advanced non-native speakers of English who are attending or will attend a university-level academic program in English and who are expected, as part of their studies, to make academic presentations. The text was classroom-tested primarily with graduate students but has also been used successfully with undergraduates. The materials were designed for presenters from a range of academic fields; discipline-specific material has been excluded. Instructors who work with international students planning to become teaching assistants (TAs) or graduate student instructors (GSIs) may also wish to consider using this book. While the text does not address teacher-student classroom interaction, it does focus on a number of skills needed for good teaching. It is, therefore, best used before a more advanced TA/GSI training course. For suggestions for using the text with pre-TAs/GSIs, see the Notes to the Instructor (available online).

Giving Academic Presentations can also be successfully used with native speakers. However, since it was written with non-native speakers in mind, instructors may have to add, eliminate, or adapt materials through a process of trial and error. Suggestions for using the text with native speakers are provided in the Notes to the Instructor (available online).

This textbook teaches skills as diverse as choosing an appropriate topic, creating effective visuals, and designing a speech opening. While some aspects of speech giving are emphasized, such as awareness and use of common speech types and organizational strategies, one important aim of the text is to make presenters aware that giving an effective presentation requires mastery of a broad range of skills.

The diversity of skills included in *Giving Academic Presentations* is reflected in a summary of its contents:

- analysis of speeches to help speakers become more aware of the thought processes involved in speech planning
- examination of major speech types and accompanying organizational strategies
- discussion of connecting devices and how they can successfully enhance the flow of a speech
- suggestions for developing speech introductions, including designing openers and choosing and organizing introductory material
- discussion of the importance of speech overviews and suggestions for designing overviews and visuals to accompany them
- ways to improve non-verbal behavior
- suggestions for speaker-listener interaction including
  - checking for understanding
  - requesting questions from the audience
  - preparing for and responding to questions from the audience
  - interrupting the speaker to ask questions or request clarification
- discussion of the importance of using evidence in academic speaking and the advantage of using certain types of evidence
- examination of ways to qualify claims and strategies to make weaker or stronger claims
- definition and discussion of fillers
- advice on preparing visuals using PowerPoint slides
- presentation of practical information about when and how to use visuals
- pronunciation work on pausing, stress, and intonation
- practical advice about preparing and practicing speeches
- opportunities for presenters to evaluate their own and others' work

The text is organized into six units, each highlighting a different speech type. A typical unit begins with a brief introduction that explains the rationale for choosing the speech type and its relevance to users of the text. Each unit includes one or more speeches to be analyzed and questions to guide the discussion. Answers to the questions are then briefly summarized. Other sections of each unit concentrate on specific speech-making skills. The final task in each unit is the presentation itself. Evaluation sheets are included. Each unit except Unit 6 contains pronunciation practice.

A number of changes have been made to the second edition.

- [ ] The format is clearer, and the contents and artwork have been updated.
- [ ] Many new tasks, as well as additional speeches and suggestion sections, have been added.
- [ ] Work with graphs and charts has been expanded.
- [ ] Information on computer projection and using PowerPoint is now included.
- [ ] Unit 2 has been expanded to cover comparison and contrast.
- [ ] Unit 6 now includes a section on presenting biographical information and an introduction to giving research presentations.

The Michigan Corpus of Academic Spoken English (MICASE)

Sections of the text, especially those related to improving speaker-listener interaction, incorporate examples from the University of Michigan English Language Institute's collection of academic spoken English, *the Michigan Corpus of Academic Spoken English (MICASE)* (R. C. Simpson, S. L. Briggs, J. Ovens, and J. M. Swales, compilers. 1999–2000. The Michigan Corpus of Academic Spoken English. Ann Arbor, MI. The Regents of the University of Michigan. Reproduced with permission of MICASE). MICASE contains speech events in various academic settings, including lectures, student and faculty panels, and one-on-one discussions. The first of its kind in the United States, this corpus is extremely useful for textbook writers because it contains language that speakers of academic English have actually spoken. Information about MICASE and currently available transcripts are available at www.elicorpora.info/.

Notes to the Instructor

The Notes to the Instructor are available online at www.press.umich.edu/elt/tm/ for use with this text. It offers both general advice on how to use the text and specific suggestions for using material in each unit. Suggestions for additional instructor-designed activities are also included.

Comments and feedback on the text can be sent to susanrei@umich.edu.

Unit 1 ──────────────

Giving an Introduction Speech

When we think about making academic presentations, we probably don't think about making introductions. However, introductions are a part of many academic situations. For example, we may introduce a new member of our department to other members. Similarly, at a national meeting or conference we often informally introduce one colleague to another. We may also find ourselves making introductions in more formal contexts, such as presenting the members of a panel discussion or introducing a speaker at a guest lecture, seminar, or conference.

We may also have to introduce ourselves. For example, we may visit advisors, professors, or mentors to share relevant background information about ourselves. Or, in a more formal setting, we might be expected to provide information about ourselves as proof of our expertise, such as when presenting a conference talk or interviewing for a research or teaching assistant (graduate student instructor) position. In this unit, you will make a presentation in which you introduce one of your classmates to the rest of the class.

Before preparing any academic speech, it is important to consider

❐ audience
❐ purpose
❐ organization

Sizing Up Your Audience

Your audience will influence how you develop your speech—from content to organization to presentation style. For speeches in class, your audience will generally consist of the other students and the instructor.

─**Discussion Questions**──────────────────────────────

1. Size up your audience. What characteristics of the audience members should you take into account when planning and presenting an introduction speech?

2. How is this audience similar to or different from one you would encounter in your own department?

Clarifying Your Purpose

The purpose of an introduction speech may vary. For instance, in a social-academic context you may want to establish a network among peers. When introducing a speaker at a conference, your purpose may be to establish the speaker's credibility.

─**Discussion Question**──────────────────────────────

1. Besides providing the opportunity for you to speak in front of the class, what might the purpose of the introduction speech in this unit be?

Organizing Your Speech

Organizing a speech is probably the single most important task of a good presenter. If your speech is well organized, the audience members will likely be able to follow you, even if your grammar and pronunciation are not totally accurate. As you work through the text, you will become familiar with several major organizational patterns in English. Depending on the type of speech you are making and the information you want to convey, these patterns will form the framework of your presentation.

Task 1: Organizing Notes

Here are some notes from an interview with an international student from Germany. How would you organize them? Working in groups, compare your strategy with those used by other members of your group.

Notes

____ Gundren Freilig — German

____ Lives with husband and daughter

____ 2007 Bach. of Sci.—envir engin

____ 2008 Intern, water mgt project

____ Langs: German, Spanish (mother from Spain), Engl.

____ Plays guitar, played in café to help pay college

____ 2009-2010 wrkd in water mgt proj in Central Amer

____ 2013 began Master's in envir engin—water resources

____ undergrad awds—academic excellence, graduated with honors

____ loves hiking with family in nat'l parks in N. Amer.

Task 2: Two Introduction Outlines

Here are outlines of two introduction speeches. Answer the questions.

1. How is Speech 1 organized?

2. Is Speech 2 organized the same way? Explain the similarities or differences.

3. Was the organizational style you used in Task 1 similar to the style used in either of these speeches?

Speech 1	Speech 2
Introduction of partner: name and country	Introduction of partner: name and country
B.S. degree (2006) 1st job—military (2006) 2nd job (2008) M.A. degree + award (2012) 3rd job (2013)	Educational background ▪ B.A. degree ▪ M.A. degree ▪ Current studies
Current studies and research assistantship ▪ major ▪ research area of interest	Work experience ▪ 1st job ▪ 2nd job ▪ current job—research assistant
Current interests ▪ family: new baby ▪ American football	Extracurricular activities ▪ Skiing ▪ Computer games
Closing	Closing

Both speakers use chronological order (arrangement of information in order of its time of occurrence from past to present) to discuss the person's educational background and work experience. However, the second speaker first uses classification (organization of information by category) to separate the person's educational background from work experience. Then, within each of these two categories, the speaker organizes information chronologically. Both speakers will likely present information about the person's current studies, interests, and extracurricular activities by listing details.

Task 3: Introducing Someone with No Work Experience

Look at the outline for a third speech. The person being introduced doesn't appear to have work experience. How does the speaker compensate for this? Which organizational patterns do you think the speaker plans to use?

Speech 3
Introduction of partner: name and country
Current studies and goals
Past educational experience
Educational accomplishments
Extracurricular activities and hobbies
Volunteer activities

Rather than beginning with a description of prior educational accomplishments and proceeding in chronological order, the speaker first focuses on the person's current academic studies and goals, placing the subject in a specific area of expertise within the academic community. Then the speaker shifts back in time to past educational experience. At this point, the speaker will likely organize information about this topic chronologically. Because the person being introduced has no work experience, the speaker chose three other categories to highlight, beginning with specific educational accomplishments, such as winning a science award. Next, the speaker discusses extracurricular activities, such as being a member of a school club or sports team, and hobbies, such as jewelry-making or building model planes. Last, the speaker mentions non-academic community volunteer work. The speaker's organizational strategy for these last three sections will likely be listing.

Flow: First Look at Connecting Devices and Topic Shifts

The organizational patterns you choose often lend themselves to the use of specific connecting or linking devices, such as time connectors (*then, after, next,* etc.) or listing words (*first, second, third, also,* etc.). These devices help maintain a smooth, coherent flow of speech, which makes it easier for the audience to follow.

Connecting devices can be used to indicate topic shifts, but topic shifts can be more elaborate, as shown in these examples.

> *You may be wondering why Andrea didn't go to college right after she graduated from high school.*
>
> *What about Yoshi's work experience?*
>
> *As for Amir's research interests, he is currently . . . .*
>
> *Now let me tell you a little about Sun's family.*
>
> *Surprisingly, Soroya's area of studies is very different from her past work experience.*

What other options might the speaker choose?

---

the following, following

In addition to words like *after, while, then, during,* and *before,* the words *the following* and *following* can be used as time connectors in speeches that are organized chronologically.

The following generally precedes a time period, such as *the following year, month,* or *week. Following,* on the other hand, generally precedes a specific event, such as *following my job as a lab technician, retirement, the birth of my child, his two-year internship,* or *high school.* Notice that the event can be an experience that takes place over a period of time.

- ☑ During my first semester of college, I majored in art. *The following semester,* however, I switched to architecture.
- ☑ *Following graduation,* Sonya had three laboratory jobs.

Task 4: Announcing Topic Shifts

Read the three excerpts. Then, with a partner, underline the connecting devices the speakers use to announce a topic shift.

Excerpts
1. Wei worked in a pharmaceutical company for three years. Now he's come back to school to get a PhD in Pharmacology so that he can teach at a university in his country. I was curious to know what Wei does in his spare time. He says he especially enjoys listening to jazz.
2. In high school, Adrienne was president of the student government for two years. She was also a member of the drama club and had the lead in three plays. When she was a senior, Adrienne got her first real job as the lead in a summer theater production. So what does Adrienne see as her future educational goals? She plans to major in Communication Studies in college.
3. Marco told me that this summer he spent a lot of time on his favorite hobby—fixing his two motorcycles. This fall, though, he's enrolled in a M.A. program in Botany at the university. His major area of interest is medicinal properties of plants. You may be surprised to know that before Marco came to the U.S. he worked as a nurse.*

*Notice that the speaker refers to the present and then shifts to the past. Why?

Organization Indicator Statements

Working in pairs or small groups, look at the slide about Sonya's work experience and read the excerpts. Then answer the questions. Notice the content is similar to the Work Experience section of the Speech 2 outline in Task 2.

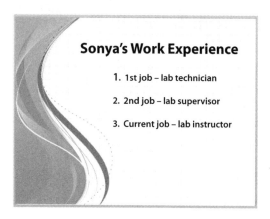

Discussion Questions

Excerpt A
Following graduation, Sonya first worked as a lab technician. . . . Then she was promoted to lab supervisor. . . . And after that, she became a lab instructor.

Excerpt B
Following graduation, Sonya had three laboratory jobs. First, she worked as a lab technician. . . . Then she was promoted to lab supervisor. . . . And after that, she became a lab instructor.

1. How are Excerpts A and B similar? Different? Which one do you prefer? Why?

2. In Excerpt B, the speaker uses an organization indicator statement, *Following graduation, Sonya had three laboratory jobs,* before listing Sonya's lab jobs. What is its purpose?

3. Would you use an organization indicator statement before these statements? Why or why not. If so, how would you word it?

   a. He enjoys dancing, surfing, and playing games with his son.

   b. He thought he wouldn't like the food here. His writing in English wasn't very good. He thought people would be unfriendly.

   c. In her department, she won first prize for the best urban park design. She won first prize for her waterfront design.

Both Excerpts A and B list Sonya's jobs in sequence by using the time connectors *first, then,* and *after that.* However, Excerpt B includes an organization indicator statement that summarizes how many jobs Sonya has had, which is an indication of how the information that follows will be organized: *Following graduation, Sonya had three laboratory jobs.* Organization indicator statements or discourse indicator statements are used frequently in academic English. They are procedural in that they tell the audience what information they can expect to hear next and give some indication about how it might be organized. They are useful when presenting lists that are composed of complete sentences, as in 3b. Organization indicator or discourse indicator statements can also be used to highlight important information, as in 3c.

Beginning Your Speech

There are a number of ways to begin your introduction speech. Some openings may be rather formulaic and others more creative. A few may seem slightly inappropriate or odd. Which of these options do you think are effective? Why? Which is grammatically correct in English? *I'm going to introduce you* [name] or *I'm going to introduce you to* [name]?

> *Today I'm happy to introduce you to* _____ *, who recently came to the university from the Czech Republic.*
>
> *Good morning. I'd like to introduce you to that girl with the brown hair over there,* _____. *She's a nurse from Bangkok, Thailand.*
>
> *My dear classmates, today I have the honor of introducing you to a nice Russian kid named* _____.
>
> *Hi, everyone. It's my pleasure to introduce you to a journalist who never expected to be studying photography. His name is* _____.
>
> *I'm pleased to introduce you to a woman who's interested in stones and bones. She's studying physical anthropology here at the university. Her name is* _____ .*

---

*Notice that the speaker begins by telling the audience what the woman's current position is. This strategy of first situating the subject in his or her present context is common and does not preclude the speaker from (1) using chronological order to organize the rest of the speech or (2) elaborating on the subject's current position later in the speech.

Concluding Your Speech

When you conclude your introduction speech, try to end on a positive note. You may rely on formulaic expressions such as

> *So let's (please) welcome . . . .*
>
> *I'm sure we'll all enjoy getting to know . . . .*
>
> *Let's give a warm welcome to . . . .*

Avoid an abrupt ending such as *So that's all* or *I'm done*.

Task 5: Gathering Information for an Introduction Speech

Working in pairs, interview your partner. Gather enough information to enable you to develop a three- to four-minute introduction speech. First, concentrate on collecting information about your partner's educational and professional experience and current academic interests. Then take some time to ask your partner about family, extracurricular activities, and other non-academic interests. If you are interviewing an undergraduate who has had little professional experience, include questions about participation in high school clubs and community organizations, awards, travel, volunteer work, and short-term jobs.

During the interview, encourage your partner to provide details about the topics you discuss. Before you end the interview, be sure you know how to pronounce your partner's name and what your partner wants members of the class to call him or her.

List the questions that you plan to ask your partner during the interview in the box. Then write the notes you collect.

QUESTIONS	NOTES

Task 6: What to Include and How Much?

Read the excerpt from the beginning of an introduction speech and decide which changes you would make. Working in small groups, answer the questions on page 12.

> The lady I'm going to introduce you to today is Carolina from San José.
> San José has about 2 million people. It's got great night life, shopping,
> and museums. Carolina lives at 30 Stone Hill Lane in case you want
> to visit her. Carolina is a first-year Master's student in the School of
> Nursing. She began to show an interest in medicine at the age of four
> when her brother stepped on her cat's tail. She responded quickly by
> bandaging the tail in adhesive tape.

─Discussion Questions─────────────────────────────

1. What information has the speaker included in this introductory excerpt that you would omit? Why?

2. What information has the speaker left out that you would include? Why?

3. Why do you think the speaker mentions the cat story? Would you keep the story or eliminate it?

In a more casual or collegial academic setting, introduce a person by both his or her first and last name (e.g., *Carolina Mendoza*) and then refer to the person by his or her first name (*Carolina*). In a more formal academic setting, also begin by saying the person's complete name (e.g., *Mohammad Aziz*). Depending on the situation, it may be appropriate to include the person's title, such as Professor, Doctor, or Dean. You may wish to ask the person how he or she would like to be referred to after your opening. However, if you feel uncomfortable calling the person by his or her first name, simply continue to use the person's title (e.g., *Dr. Aziz*). Men with no specific title can be referred to as *Mr.* and women as *Ms.,* unless they prefer *Miss* or *Mrs.*

Avoid referring to the person you introduce as *lady, girl, gal, kid,* or *guy,* even in an informal setting. These references are not considered appropriate. Instead, use *person, woman,* or *man.*

Focus on the academic and professional information you gathered. To avoid embarrassing your partner, (1) exclude personal information, such as phone number, address, and age, and (2) avoid references to the person's physical attributes, such as how attractive he or she is. Instead, use adjectives that might describe academic and/or professional attributes, such as *talented* or *creative*. Other adjectives that may aptly describe your partner include *industrious, promising, enthusiastic,* and *versatile.* Be sure to provide details to support your use of the adjective.

Include background information that the audience might need. For example, rather than simply saying San José, use the complete geographical location (*San José, Costa Rica,* or *San José, the capital of Costa Rica*).

Remove information that shifts the focus away from the person you're introducing, such as *San José has about 2 million people. It's got great nightlife, shopping, and museums.*

Sometimes speakers plan to use humor in their presentation; other times it arises spontaneously from the circumstances. When using humor, keep your audience, purpose, and relationship to the person you're introducing in mind. If used appropriately, humor can heighten audience interest, which in turn may make you feel more relaxed. If you know the person well, you may want to tell a humorous anecdote about that person to provide a more personal touch as well as serve as a lead-in to a section of your introduction.

Task 7: Introducing Colleagues at Lectures and Conferences

At academic lectures and conferences, a guest speaker may be introduced to the audience by one of the organizers or moderators of the event. In this situation, the guest speaker, James Hilton, is being introduced by the director of the Language Resource Center at the University of Michigan, Monika Dressler, at a conference called "Integrating Teaching, Information, and Technology." It was designed for faculty members at the university.

Read the introduction and then, with a partner, answer the questions on page 14. Sentence numbers have been added for your convenience.

① The title of this opening event is "Two Sides of the Technology Coin: Perspectives on Enhancing Student Learning and Supporting Faculty Scholarship." ② Our first speaker will present on the first side of the coin–that of enhancing student learning. ③ James Hilton is an Arthur F. Thurnau Professor* and the undergraduate chair in Psychology at the University of Michigan. ④ He received his undergraduate degree in Psychology from the University of Texas in 1981 and his PhD from the social psychology program at Princeton University in 1985. ⑤ Among the courses he teaches are Introductory Psychology, Introductory Social Psychology, and Experimental Methods. ⑥ These courses range in size from 25 to 1,200 students. ⑦ He is a three-time recipient of the LS&A Excellence in Education Award at the University of Michigan, and (although he doesn't look all that old) he is also the recipient of the Class of 1923 Memorial Teaching Award. ⑧ His research focuses on expectancy effects, stereotypes, and the psychology of suspicion. ⑨ Along with Charles Perdue, he is the author of a multimedia CD-ROM in psychology entitled *Longman Mind Matters* published by Addison Wesley Longman. ⑩ Whew . . . that's his official introduction. ⑪ To add to this are some adjectives that some of my staff and student workers volunteered: *dynamic, entertaining, dedicated, multifaceted, innovative, funny,* and *really smart.* ⑫ It is my immense pleasure to welcome our first speaker, James Hilton.

(Introduction by Monika Dressler, with slight modifications.)

---

*U.S. university professors are distinguished by being given a position that has the name of a former outstanding scholar or contributor.

──**Discussion Questions**────────────────────

1. What information is included in this introduction? What details about the speaker interested you?

2. How is the introduction organized?

3. Did the speaker use any connecting devices? Explain and give examples and locations.

4. Explain how this introduction takes into account the purpose and the audience.

Notice that the speaker depends less on chronological order than on classification to organize information. Categories she highlights are current teaching responsibilities and awards, research and publications, and praise from colleagues and students. The speaker generally relies on listing to organize information within categories. She uses the connecting device, *to add to this* in Sentence 11.

Task 8: Introducing a Guest Speaker

At a yearly lecture, Abigail Stewart, Director of the Institute for Research on Women and Gender at the University of Michigan, gave this introduction* of an invited speaker from Cornell University. Read the introduction and then, working in small groups, answer the questions on page 15.

> I'm Abby Stewart, Director of the Institute for Research on Women and Gender. My special job and pleasure is to welcome Joan Brumberg to Ann Arbor and to tell you a little bit about her before she tells us about *The Body Project*. One indicator of the range and breadth of Professor Brumberg's knowledge and expertise is the fact that she is currently the Steven Weiss Presidential Fellow and Professor of History, Human Development, and Women's Studies at Cornell University.
>
> She's taught at Cornell since completing her education at the University of Rochester, Boston College, and the University of Virginia. Most of us in this room know Professor Brumberg as

───────────
*Abridged from MICASE, with minor changes.

the author of *The Body Project, An Intimate History of American Girls.* She has truly distinguished herself as an authority, both on the experience of adolescence among girls and the particular developmental vulnerabilities girls face. The hallmark of her work is the combination of rich psychological insight, acute social analysis, and creative historical research with a beautiful writing style.

Professor Brumberg has been recognized by a Guggenheim Fellowship and grants from the National Endowment for the Humanities and Rockefeller Foundation. She has worked on a number of public history projects—she's consulted on a film project on the history of the Girl Scouts, an exhibit on the history of asylums in New York state, and an historical site interpretation for museum educators. She's currently working on a project on girls' diaries.

Linda Kerber was correct when she wrote on the book jacket [of *The Body Project*] that Joan Jacobs Brumberg tells a stunning and troubling story. What is even more important, though, is that she has some important ideas about how we might do better in providing what adolescent girls need to survive. So, now I'd like to welcome her to the lectern so you can hear what she has to say.

Discussion Questions

1. What's the specific purpose of this event? How are the goals of the event in Task 7 different?

2. What's different about the invited speakers?

3. Is the audience the same or different from the audience in Task 7? Explain.

4. In this presentation, what topics does the introducer cover? How are they similar to or different from the topics covered in Task 7?

5. The introduction in Task 7 is about two-thirds as long as the introduction in Task 8, which was originally twice as long, but has been abridged. Why is this introduction so much longer? Does it have to do with the invited speaker, the audience, or the purpose of the event?

6. Discuss how the purpose of an event determines how an introduction is designed and what information is included.

The event in the Task 7 focuses on teaching through technology, one area of the guest speaker's expertise. The audience members are faculty members—in other words, the speaker's colleagues. To increase interest in the speaker, the introducer lists some of his appealing qualities. The event in Task 8 is a yearly lecture given by a well-known scholar from another university. Her extensive research on adolescent women is, in part, demonstrated by the book she will discuss. The audience members, who likely have heard of the speaker or have read her work, may include students and faculty from the Women's Studies Department as well as members from other departments and local citizens. The information included in both introductions is linked to the purpose of the event. The length of the presentation in Task 8 likely has to do with the goals of the introducer—to honor the speaker and to acknowledge and offer evidence of the speaker's standing and expertise.

Task 9: Introducing a Speaker at a Conference

Imagine that you have been asked to introduce a well-known professor at your university or an internationally known speaker from your field of studies. In preparing your speech, you may include things like

- degrees
- recent work history and current work
- current research interests
- publications
- awards and other accomplishments
- praise from others about the speaker

Before concluding your introduction, be sure to include the title of the speaker's presentation.

Task 10: Overcoming Nervousness

Everyone is somewhat nervous when speaking before a group for the first time, but nervousness will diminish as you have more opportunities to make presentations. Place a check mark (✔) next to the concerns from the list that you have now. Throughout the course, you will be able to address these concerns with your instructor and other members of the class.

_____ 1. I'm worried that other students won't understand me because of my pronunciation.

_____ 2. I think I'll forget what I want to say when I stand in front of a group.

_____ 3. I feel uncomfortable making eye contact with the audience.

_____ 4. I think the other students will be bored because I speak slowly in English.

_____ 5. I've been told I talk too fast.

_____ 6. I am afraid that I will not be able to express myself clearly.

Write one or two other concerns you have and share them with a partner or small group.

_____ 7. _____

_____ 8. _____

Tips for Overcoming Nervousness

> ❯ Practice your speech so that you feel in control of the contents.

> ❯ Ask a friend or family member to listen to your speech and give feedback.

> ❯ If possible, set up the classroom the way you would like it. Stand where you can see all the members of the audience.

> ❯ Keep your hands free so that you can gesture. Gesturing helps you look and feel more confident.

> ❯ If you are worried that you will forget information, put a small piece of paper with notes in your hand or on a table next to you. Quickly review it before your speech.

> ❯ Distract yourself by thinking of something unrelated to your speech, such as what you ate for breakfast.

> ❯ Take several deep breaths before starting.

> ❭ Begin at a slow pace. Don't rush.

> ❭ Project your voice. A strong voice can give you confidence and convince the audience that you have control over your topic.

> ❭ Act confident. Maintain eye contact and a friendly attitude toward the audience. Try smiling when you start your introduction.

> ❭ If you are really nervous, you may get some relief by telling the audience that you are nervous, especially if you are in an informal setting with your peers.

Non-Verbal Behavior

Because of your concerns about speaking in front of an audience, you may unknowingly engage in behavior that detracts from your speech.

Avoiding eye contact with the audience
- ❑ looking at the ceiling, out the window, at the floor, or at the camera
- ❑ staring at one member of the audience or at only one section of the room
- ❑ looking at notes to avoid eye contact with the audience

Avoiding friendly facial expressions
- ❑ maintaining a serious, unchanging facial expression

Making distracting body movements
- ❑ pulling on your sleeve
- ❑ pacing back and forth or shuffling your feet
- ❑ moving your hands in and out of your pockets
- ❑ slapping your hand on the side of your leg
- ❑ playing with objects in your hand (paper, pens, keys, etc.)
- ❑ touching your hair or face

Avoiding the use of hand gestures
- ❑ grasping your hands behind your back or in front of you
- ❑ keeping your hands in your pockets or "glued" to your side
- ❑ holding something in your hand, such as a pen, large piece of paper, or pointer

Other distracting behaviors
- ❑ laughing nervously
- ❑ chewing or snapping gum

Tips for Improving Non-Verbal Communication

> ❯ Hand gestures will be discussed more fully in Unit 4. In the meantime, keep your hands empty of unnecessary objects and avoid grasping or hiding your hands. By doing so, your hands will be left free to gesture naturally.

> ❯ If you think you may have trouble establishing eye contact with the audience or tend to focus on only one or two listeners, try dividing the audience into three or four groups. Move your eyes from one group to another, making sure to include the groups to your far left and far right. If you feel uncomfortable looking directly at people's eyes, look at another part of their face, such as their nose.

> ❯ Try to maintain a friendly, relaxed relationship with your audience. Listeners will respond positively to your show of confidence.

Task 11: Preparing and Delivering Your Speech

Read these approaches to preparing and delivering your speech. Choose the ones you would use to help you prepare and deliver a speech. Discuss your responses with a partner.

_____ 1. Checking the accuracy of your information

_____ 2. Writing your speech word for word

_____ 3. Reading your speech

_____ 4. Memorizing your speech word for word

_____ 5. Preparing notes on a small note card and using the note card if you forget what you were going to say

_____ 6. Practicing your speech once in advance, assuming you'll do a good job when you get to class

_____ 7. Practicing your speech silently in your head

_____ 8. Rehearsing and timing your speech five to six times in front of a mirror

_____ 9. Recording your speech before class and then evaluating yourself

The Importance of Practice

Practice your speech three times orally, standing in front of a mirror. Then record it one or two times and evaluate yourself. Make changes and practice again. Ask a colleague or friend to listen to you and give you feedback. Practice will help you feel better prepared and thus more confident. You will have fewer pauses and will be able to remember the contents of your speech better, making it possible to speak with no notes or a small note card. Practice will also help you avoid translating from your native language.

When you practice, keep in mind that minor grammar errors generally don't interfere with the audience's ability to understand you. Also, if you forget to include a few details, the audience probably won't be aware of those omissions.

Pronunciation

Pausing

During their speeches, some presenters speak too slowly and haltingly, while others speak too quickly. Both of these problems can be avoided with proper pausing.

- **Speaking too slowly.**

   When presenters pause too often, they seem unprepared because their presentations are slow and choppy. This may be because they pause after every word or two. If you think you pause too much, one helpful suggestion is to practice more. When practicing, try to say a group of several words before pausing. That way, the speech flow will seem smoother to the listener. The more confident you become, the less you will pause and the longer your groupings will be. Some natural groups of words include time expressions, subject + verb + object, prepositional phrases, longer noun phrases, and main and subordinate clauses.

Example	Grouping
Now,*	time expression (adverb)
John's studying business	subject + verb + object
at the University of Michigan	prepositional phrase
His major area of interest	noun phrase
[is] managing non-profit corporations	noun phrase
Before John went to college,	subordinate clause
he traveled around the world for two years	main clause

*Speakers may find it useful to pause slightly after adverbs that function as connecting devices, such as *currently, consequently, however,* and *nevertheless.*

What is pausing? In this section, pauses are defined in two ways.

1. **When the speaker makes a complete stop.** Speakers may come to a complete stop at the end of a sentence, for example, to take a breath or to begin a topic shift, as in

   John's major area of interest is managing non-profit corporations. (Pause stop) Before John went to college, he traveled around the world for two years.

2. **When the speaker rests, slows down, or lingers at a particular point, such as at the end of the word grouping.** Because the speaker slows down but does not stop, the word before the pause is linked to the word after the pause, as in

   Before John went to college (pause slow down), he traveled around the world for two years.

   In this example, the speaker slows down at *college* and then links it to the next word, *he.* The word *college* is slightly extended or lengthened and then flows into *he (college͡he).**

Read this passage out loud. Slow down after the groupings marked with //. Link the word before the pause to the word that follows. Make a complete stop after groupings marked with ///. Try to minimize rather than eliminate other pauses.

Right now, // John's studying business // at the University of Michigan. /// His major area of interest // is managing nonprofit corporations. /// Before John went to college, // he traveled around the world for two years. ///

- **Speaking too quickly.**
  Presenters who speak too quickly have a tendency to forget to pause at the end of natural word groupings in English. This puts extra demands on listeners who need time to absorb information. Speakers who speak too quickly can modify their speed by consciously pausing at the end of a word grouping.

---

*In American English, the *h* is not generally pronounced when *he* is unstressed.

Task 12: Using Pauses in Your Introduction Speech

Fill in the blanks with information about yourself. Mark the places where you will slow down (//) or stop (///). Then practice saying the information out loud with a partner.

Hi. My name's _____ and I come from _____.

Right now I'm studying (working as) _____

in the _____. My main area of

interest is _____.

Before I came here, I _____

_____. My future plans

are to _____

_____.

Task 13: Evaluating Pauses

At home, practice and record the paragraph in Task 12. Evaluate yourself. Indicate where you paused. Do you think that you paused too little or too much? If you think you paused too much, practice grouping words together and pausing after each grouping. Try to minimize rather than eliminate pauses. If you think you spoke too quickly, add pauses after natural word groupings and say the sentences again. If you still find yourself speaking too quickly, try taking a breath or saying "pause" to yourself at natural breaks before continuing. Come to a full stop, especially when making a topic shift. Record yourself again and compare the two performances.

Task 14: Introduction Presentation

Prepare a short three- to four-minute formal introduction of a new partner. First, interview your partner. Then decide what information you would like to include in your speech. Be sure to find out how you can contact your partner in case you need additional information.

1. Carefully organize your speech, using one or more of the organizing patterns you've studied.

2. Use connecting devices and topic shift indicators to link parts of your speech to each other and make smooth transitions.

3. Plan a short introduction and conclusion. In your introduction, you may first wish to tell the audience your partner's current academic or professional position and then discuss the events that led to it.

4. Follow general statements with specific details that enhance audience interest.

5. If you think you will forget your speech, make a small note card with your outline on it. A large piece of paper may distract attention from the audience. Don't read your speech or memorize it word for word. Instead, refer to the note card to help you remember what you are going to say.

Introduction Speech Outline

(Put your outline on a note card about this size.)

6. Practice your speech two to three times by standing and reading it out loud. Pay attention to non-verbal behavior that may detract from or enhance your speech. Then record your speech. Listen to your presentation and decide what sections need improvement. Use the evaluation form on pages 24–25 as a guide. Then practice your speech several more times. Ask a colleague or friend to listen to your speech and give you feedback.

Introduction Speech Evaluation

Listen to your final speech. Then complete the Introduction Speech Evaluation Form. Be sure to provide specific comments in the Comments section. Also, set goals for your next speech.

If you would like to evaluate your speech with one or two partners, discuss your strengths and weaknesses and then complete the evaluation form. If you wish, include feedback from your partners on the form.

A sample completed evaluation is provided on pages 26–27.

Introduction Speech Evaluation Form

Name: _____

	(Make a check in the appropriate column)			
	Good	OK	Needs Work	Comments (include specific problems you noticed)
Topic information Interesting details? Suitable for this audience?				
Introduction Adequate? Attention-getting?				
Organization Clear organizational strategy? Used organization indicator statement(s) when appropriate?				
Flow Smooth, coherent speech flow? Used appropriate connecting devices and topic shift markers?				
Conclusion Adequate? Smooth, not abrupt?				
Eye contact and facial expressions Focus on the audience? Contact with all members of the audience? Friendly facial expression?				

	(Make a check in the appropriate column)			
	Good	OK	Needs Work	Comments (include specific problems you noticed)
Gestures and other body movements Hands free and expressive? Body posture relaxed rather than stiff? No distracting body movements?				
Voice Good volume? Confident? Relaxed?				
Pace Not too fast or too slow? Smooth rather than halting or hesitant?				
Pronunciation (specific problems)				
Other comments				
Goals for my next presentation (list 2–3 areas that you want to improve for your next presentation)				

Sample Completed Evaluation

<table>
<tr><th colspan="5" style="text-align:center">Introduction Speech Evaluation Form</th></tr>
<tr><td colspan="5">Name: _____</td></tr>
<tr><td></td><td colspan="3" style="text-align:center">(Make a check in the appropriate column)</td><td></td></tr>
<tr><td></td><td>Good</td><td>OK</td><td>Needs Work</td><td>Comments (include specific problems you noticed)</td></tr>
<tr>
<td>Topic information
Interesting details?
Suitable for this audience?</td>
<td></td><td>✓</td><td></td>
<td>It was pretty good, but I should have given more details about my partner's work experience.</td>
</tr>
<tr>
<td>Introduction
Adequate?
Attention-getting?</td>
<td>✓</td><td></td><td></td>
<td>Good. I used a little humor.</td>
</tr>
<tr>
<td>Organization
Clear organizational strategy?
Used organization indicator statement(s) when appropriate?</td>
<td>✓</td><td></td><td></td>
<td>I organized by chronological order and used an organization indicator statement <u>Juan has had two research positions at the university.</u></td>
</tr>
<tr>
<td>Flow
Smooth, coherent speech flow?
Used appropriate connecting devices and topic shift markers?</td>
<td>✓</td><td></td><td></td>
<td>I think I successfully used time connectors.
I used <u>as for</u> in <u>As for his family.</u></td>
</tr>
<tr>
<td>Conclusion
Adequate?
Smooth, not abrupt?</td>
<td></td><td>✓</td><td></td>
<td>Good, but at the end I said, <u>I'm finished.</u> It wasn't necessary.</td>
</tr>
<tr>
<td>Eye contact and facial expressions
Focus on the audience?
Contact with all members of the audience?
Friendly facial expression?</td>
<td></td><td></td><td>✓</td>
<td>I hardly looked at the audience because I was nervous. I looked at my notes even though I didn't need them.</td>
</tr>
<tr>
<td>Gestures and other body movements
Hands free and expressive?
Body posture relaxed rather than stiff?
No distracting body movements?</td>
<td></td><td>✓</td><td></td>
<td>I moved my right hand but kept my left hand in my pocket.</td>
</tr>
</table>

	(Make a check in the appropriate column)			
	Good	OK	Needs Work	Comments (include specific problems you noticed)
Voice Good volume? Confident? Relaxed?			✓	My voice was too soft. Both partners said it was a little hard to hear me.
Pace Not too fast or too slow? Smooth rather than halting or hesitant?	✓			I practiced a lot, so I didn't have a lot of pauses.

Pronunciation

(specific problems)   two thousand (2000) – I said two tousand

Other comments

I wore my jacket during my speech. It wasn't necessary.

Goals for my next presentation (list 2–3 areas that you want to improve for your next presentation)

1. Include more details to keep the audience's attention
2. Use more eye contact
3. Speak louder

Unit 2 —————————————————————————————

Describing and Comparing Objects

Describing and comparing objects in an academic setting are familiar tasks. As a part of class or laboratory discussion, instructors and students frequently describe the characteristics and function of important objects in their fields of study and compare and contrast these objects with other related ones. Students may also speak about objects in a more formal setting, such as a presentation, research project discussion, or conference.

What does the term *object* mean? In this unit, *object* is used broadly. It is perhaps best explained by providing examples in somewhat informally arranged categories. For instance, objects may be animate, such as a butterfly or a tree, or inanimate, such as a microscope or suspension bridge. Objects may be part of a larger object or system, such as a computer keyboard or an eye. Many objects, such as a parasite or an atom, cannot be seen by the unaided eye. Some objects are well known to the listener, such as an antenna, while other objects, such as an oscilloscope or a machining center, may be known mainly to listeners in a particular field. Certain objects, like a pagoda or a totem pole, are familiar to listeners from one part of the world but unfamiliar to listeners from another part. Some objects may consist mainly of a written text with standard parts such as a receipt, lease, job application, cover letter, lab report, case study, government document, or drug insert.

In certain academic disciplines—such as Architecture, Engineering, Astronomy, Computer Science, Biological and Medical Sciences, Geology, and Dentistry—discussing concrete objects or instruments is far more common than in others (such as Economics, Linguistics, Sociology, Women's Studies, and Public Policy) that focus on more abstract concepts. This unit will prepare you to describe and compare objects related to your field as well as prepare you to

- ❏ work within the confines of the speech type
- ❏ choose an appropriate topic for a general academic audience

28

- [ ] decide what information to include in your presentation based on factors such as audience and time limits
- [ ] choose an organizational strategy and connecting devices that best suit your object(s)
- [ ] explain the function or purpose of the object and its specific parts
- [ ] make one or more visuals to accompany your speech

Think of the names of several objects from your field. If your field deals mainly with abstract concepts, write the names of written material that you use in your daily activities or an area unique to professionals in your field. As you go through the tasks in the unit, evaluate these objects as possible topics for your final presentation for Unit 2.

Part 1: Describing an Object

Task 1: The Receipt Speech

This unit begins with a presentation by an international student in the field of Economics in which he describes an object. While the field of Economics generally deals with more abstract concepts and principles, the topic of this speech is an object that everyone is familiar with.

Working with a partner or in a small group, read the speech entitled Receipt. Then answer the questions on page 31.

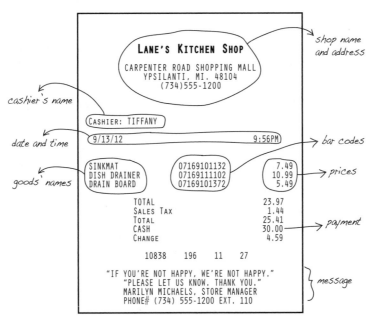

Receipt

① Hello, everybody.

② Today I'm talking about an object related to my major. My major is economics, and almost every economic transaction is ended by getting or giving receipts. So I'll talk about what kind of information we can see on a receipt. Let me talk about it from the top to the bottom of the receipt.

③ I think you may get receipts every day, but I suppose you don't look at the details of this, so I think it's valuable to explain what kind of information is on the receipt.

④ *(Points to the object on the screen)* First, as you can see, this is the name of the shop, store, you know, Lane's. It's a famous store in town. And this part has very basic information–name and address and phone number so you can see where you get, you bought those goods, from what store.

⑤ *(Points)* And next, the cashier's name is written here. It's important because for the store they can know who is responsible for this transaction. Okay?

⑥ *(Points)* And next is the date and time. These are important for both store and shopper.

⑦ *(Points)* Below this, these are the items I bought the other day–three items. This is the name of goods–in this case, sink mat. *(Points to* "sinkmat"*)*

⑧ *(Points)* And this is the bar code. Each good has its unique bar code. This bar code is not important for buyers, but it is very important for sellers because they manage, ah, they control what goods are sold or what goods remain in the store by checking these codes.

⑨ *(Points)* And this is the price, the most concerned part. And below that there is the total price and tax. And this, how I paid. In this case, I paid by cash. If I pay by a credit credit card, I think this says "Charge." So this is the information of the payment.

⑩ And I don't know this part, what it stands for. *(Points to the numbers under the word* Change*)*

⑪ *(Points)* And the final part is a message from supermarket to customers. Customers don't need this information, uh, so often, but I think this is important for the seller because in this case this message says how much they are concerned with their reputation or customers, how much they care about their customers. *(Points to and reads writing)* In this case, "If you are not happy, we're not happy. Please let us know. Thank you." So if there's any complaint on this store, please let us know. If the customers see this, they think the shop, the store, cares about us.

⑫ I think is this is a good example for explaining what a receipt is. Thank you.

(Speech by Shuichi Matsuta, with minor modifications.)

Discussion Questions

1. What is the topic and purpose of the speech? Is the topic appropriate for a general academic audience?

2. How does the speaker introduce his topic?

3. What organization strategy does he use? How do you know?

4. How does the speaker maintain the flow of his speech? Underline the words the speaker uses to move from one part of the receipt to another. How does the speaker indicate that he has reached the last section of the receipt?

5. What words does the speaker define in his speech?

6. The speaker doesn't actually give a formal definition of the word *receipt*. Why not?

7. Do you think the speaker's visual is effective? Why or why not?

8. What suggestion(s) would you give the speaker for improving his speech?

The speaker begins his speech by putting the topic into an academic context–the field of Economics. Then he introduces his topic (receipt) and tells the audience how he has organized the speech: he will talk about the parts of the receipt from top to bottom. This strategy makes it easy for him to remember what he is going to say next and for his audience to follow him. To maintain the flow of his speech, he uses connecting devices *first, and this is, below this, and next,* and *the final part.*

In this speech, the speaker does not begin with a formal definition of the word *receipt.* Nor does he define *transaction* and *goods.* He likely assumes the audience is familiar with these terms or will understand their meaning from the context. However, as he goes through the parts of the receipt, he does define several terms he thinks the audience may not be familiar with: *Lane's, bar code,* and *charge.* So, in preparing his speech, he keeps in mind what information the audience may need.

The speaker chooses a simple visual for his speech, an actual receipt. While it is not flashy or colorful, it is a clear representation of an object that everyone in the audience is familiar with but which they may have paid little attention to.

This receipt represents one of millions of small economic transactions that together have an impact on our society. If the speaker had more time, he could reiterate the importance of receipts in his conclusion.

Organization

In the Receipt speech, the speaker organized his speech spatially from top to bottom. In English, four common ways to organize a presentation on an object are

- ❏ from general to specific (or vice versa)
- ❏ spatially
- ❏ from the most important part to the least important part (or vice versa)
- ❏ logically

Keep in mind that speakers may combine several organizational strategies.

1. From General to Specific (or vice versa)

An object may consist of several major parts. The speaker first introduces the object and then each of its major parts. After that, the speaker returns to each part and describes it in detail, including its subparts. Or, the speaker may begin with the specifics before.

2. Spatially

An object may have a form or function that lends itself to a specific spatial organizational strategy. The ways to organize spatially include

- ❏ top to bottom (preferred)* or bottom to top
- ❏ left to right (preferred)* or right to left
- ❏ front to back
- ❏ outside to inside or inside to outside
- ❏ clockwise or counterclockwise

3. From the Most Important Part to the Least Important Part (or vice versa)

The speaker may wish to highlight the most important parts of the object and then discuss other relevant but less important parts. Or the speaker may begin with the less important parts and move toward the more important ones.

4. Logically

In order to explain one part of an object to the audience, the speaker may need to explain another part first. The relationship between the parts of the object may best be shown using this strategy.

---

*Speakers may prefer these because English is read from left to right, top to bottom. However, the object itself may reveal the best spatial strategy.

Task 2: Choosing an Organizational Pattern

Working in groups, look at the objects on this page and page 35. If you were giving a speech describing one of these objects, which organizational pattern (patterns) would you choose? Why? Where would you begin? How would you proceed?

Fig. 2.1. Harp

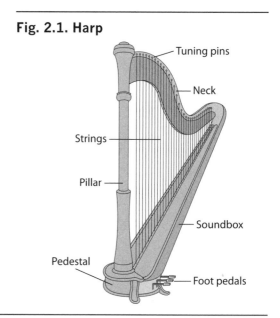

Fig. 2.2. Tree

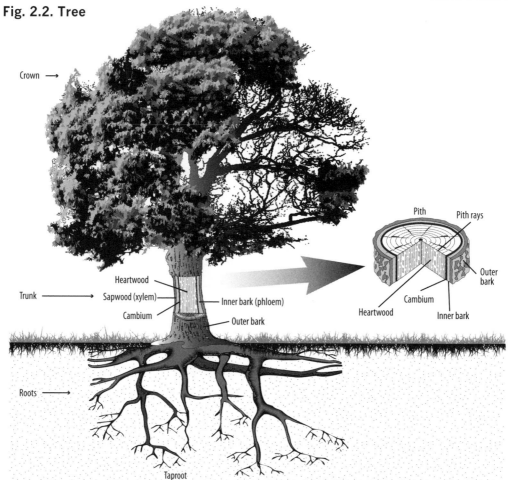

Fig. 2.3. Eye

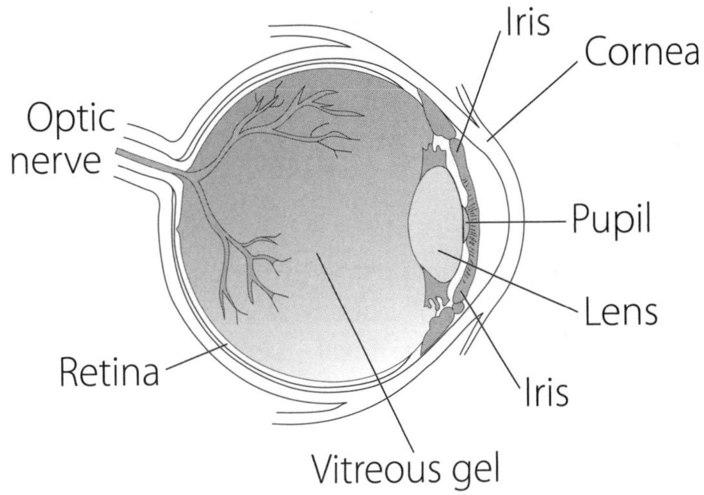

Iris
Cornea
Optic nerve
Pupil
Lens
Retina
Iris
Vitreous gel

Fig. 2.4. Wind Turbine

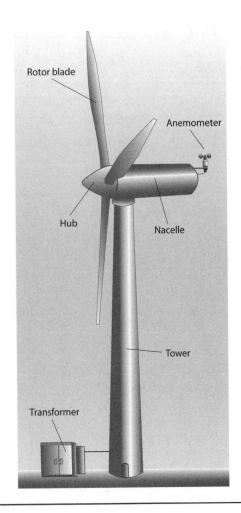

Rotor blade
Anemometer
Hub
Nacelle
Tower
Transformer

Task 3: Comparing Your Organizational Strategy

Read the proposal for a speech about the harp. What strategy is proposed? Is it similar to or different from your group's strategy? Keep in mind that there may be several ways to organize the information.

The Harp

① First, I'll introduce and define the harp so that people will know what kind of musical instrument it is: "A harp is a stringed instrument with a large triangular frame made of wood." Here I'll add more background information, for example, that it's the oldest stringed instrument, etc.

② Then I'll move to the parts. I'll begin with the *pedestal, pillar,* and *neck,* since they are the column that provides the main support for the instrument.

③ After that, I'll introduce the *strings,* since they create the unique sound of the instrument. I'll mention the number of strings and the type of sound they make.

④ Next, I'll talk about the *pins.* I can't mention the pins until I've talked about the strings because the pins are used to tune the strings.

⑤ Last, I'll discuss the *soundboard* and *pedals,* since they enhance the sound of the strings and provide additional frame support.

Pointing with Words

In English, speakers use both gestures and words to point to, introduce, or name an object and its parts. Here are some ways to point with words.

❑ One of the most common ways of introducing an object is by using *This is.*

This is a harp.

The article *a* is generally used to first introduce an object, as in *This is a harp.* Once the harp is introduced, it may be referred to as *a harp, the harp* or *harps.* The parts of the object can also be introduced by *These are.*

These are the strings.

However, the article *the* is generally used instead of *a* to introduce the various parts of the object unless the speaker is pointing out more than one of a particular part—for example, *this is a* purchase, and *this (that) is also a* purchase.

❑ Another common way to point to the parts of an object in English is by using the expression *Here you have.*

Here you have the pins, which are used to tune the strings.

❑ The expression *That is (That's)* is also commonly used when the speaker wishes to spatially relate one part of an object to another. This may indicate that the part is farther away from the previously mentioned part or from the speaker. Or it may simply be a way of distinguishing one part from another.

This is the pupil (of the eye), and *that's* the lens (right behind the pupil).*

This is can be accompanied by *here* and *that is* by *there.*

This is the cornea *here* and *that's* the retina *there.*

❑ Speakers can also name a part by using the expression *is (are) called.*

And this (that) *is called* the tower.

❑ Spatial connectors such as *next* and *after that* and prepositions of location such as *behind, underneath, in back of, next to,* or *inside of* are also used to introduce parts and relate them to each other.**

And *next* is the nacelle.

This is the outer bark of the tree, and *behind it* |is | the
inner bark.*** |you can see|

                                       |you have |

---

*And is used in this example and in the next three examples to move the discussion from one part of the object to another.

**In the Receipt speech in Task 1, the speaker used *next* as a spatial connector, as in *next is the date and time.* It is interesting to note that *then* cannot be used as a spatial connector with *be* but can be used with *you have* or *you can see (then you have, then you can see,* but not *then is).*

***In English we frequently highlight new information by putting it at the end of the sentence. In this case, the new information is the next part of the tree to be introduced. Therefore, it is less likely that we would say *This is the outer bark of the tree, and the inner bark is behind it.*

Non-Verbal Behavior: Pointing with Your Hands

Some speakers use a pointing device when introducing the parts of an object. These devices may not be necessary and can even be distracting. For example, a pointer with a red light must be held steady. Otherwise, it can bounce around so that it isn't clear what the speaker is pointing to. When possible, many effective speakers point with their hand. This strategy can help the speaker look more natural and dynamic.

One frequently asked question is, *Where should the speaker stand when using a projection device?* If speakers stand to the left or right of the screen directly facing the audience, they can gesture more easily at the object on the screen and will be in a better position to make eye contact with members of the audience. Otherwise, they may block information on the screen or be tempted to read from their computer screen, rather than maintaining eye contact with the audience.

Using Adjectives to Describe an Object

There are a number of ways to describe an object or its parts. One common way is to describe its shape *(triangular, square, round, heart-shaped, curved, wavy, oblong, spiral)*. Another is to mention the material it is made of *(wood, metal, plastic, rubber, glass)*. A third way is to use adjectives that describe its characteristics, such as *flexible, pliable, coarse, rough, smooth, thin, heavy, woven, fragile, sticky, slimy, delicate, shiny, transparent,* and *soft*. In more informal contexts, the speaker may also choose to use somewhat less "academic" but more colorful adjectives such as *humongous, nasty, teensy,* and *fluffy*.

Choose one or several objects from your field, and write some words that describe the object or some of its parts. Share them with a partner.

Statements of Purpose

When describing an object, one of the speaker's goals is to explain the purpose or function of both the object and its parts, especially if the audience is unfamiliar with them. Take a body part, such as an eye. The general purpose of the eye may be known to the audience, but the purpose of the retina, cornea, and lens may not be. Two common ways to express purpose are to use

❏ formal definitions
❏ terms that express purpose or function

Formal Definitions

Formal definitions generally consist of three parts: the term (in this case, the object), the class the term belongs to, and the term's essential differences or distinguishing characteristics. One essential difference or distinguishing characteristic of an object may be its function or purpose, as shown here. (See Unit 4 for further discussion of formal definitions.)

Essential differences/distinguishing
Term   *Class*   *characteristics (function/purpose)*
   ↓   ↓   ↓
A bar code is an electronic signal that's used to track the product.

Terms That Express Purpose or Function

In addition to using a formal definition, there are a number of ways to express purpose in spoken academic English.

Term	Example
1. **Term** *functions as* + NOUN	1. **The cornea** functions as a protective cover for the lens.
2. *The purpose (function) of* **term** *is to* + VERB (infinitive)	2. One purpose of the **outer bark** is to protect the tree from injury.
3. **Term(s)** + VERB (present simple)	3. **The pedestal, pillar, and neck** (of the harp) provide the main support.
4. **Term** *is used to* + VERB (infinitive)	4. **The pedals** are used to enhance the sound of the harp.
5. **Term** *is for* + VERB + *-ing* (gerund)	5. **The pins** are for tuning the strings.
6. *What* **term** *does is* (cleft sentence with *what* + infinitive)*	6. What **the pupil** does is (to) allow light to enter the eye.

*See Unit 3 for a discussion of cleft sentences.

Organization Indicator Statements

When preparing your object speech, keep in mind that organization indicator statements can be an effective means of notifying the audience of upcoming information and how the information is likely to be organized. (See Unit 1, page 8.) For example, an organization indicator can be used to tell the audience

❏ how many major parts you have divided the object into

> *Trees consist of three major parts—the crown, the trunk, and the roots.*

❏ how many purposes of an object you will discuss

> *The cornea has two main purposes. One* is to . . . . The other* is. . .*

Task 4: Defining School Objects

Working in pairs, define a few of these common objects using a formal three-part definition or one of the other ways mentioned in the *Terms That Express Purpose or Function* section on page 39. Compare your definitions with those of other members of your class. If you like, add a few terms from your own field of study.

blackboard eraser	keyboard
flash (thumb) drive	scissors
ballpoint pen	handout
ruler	stapler
chalk	calculator
paper clip	highlighter
projection screen	rubber band
backpack	planner

---

*See pages 141–42 in Unit 5 for a discussion of listing connectors like *one . . . the other*.

Making Visuals

For your presentation, you may be able bring the object you are going to describe to class. More likely, you will need to make at least one slide or other representation of the object you've chosen. Using computer projection, you can project images available on the web as well as your own images. You may also be able to scan images from magazines, books, journals, and encyclopedias or from your own drawing but remember to be respectful of copyright. Using a software program, you might be able to modify an image before projecting it.

Task 5: Knowing Where and How to Modify a Visual

Here is the original picture of the tree in Task 2 on page 34. Compare the two drawings. What modifications did the speaker make in Task 2? How do these modifications make the visual more effective?

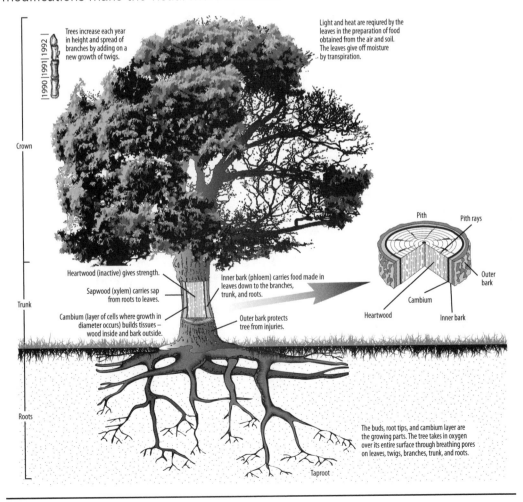

Trees increase each year in height and spread of branches by adding on a new growth of twigs.

1990 | 1991 | 1992

Light and heat are reqiured by the leaves in the preparation of food obtained from the air and soil. The leaves give off moisture by transpiration.

Crown

Pith

Pith rays

Outer bark

Heartwood (inactive) gives strength.

Sapwood (xylem) carries sap from roots to leaves.

Inner bark (phloem) carries food made in leaves down to the branches, trunk, and roots.

Cambium

Trunk

Cambium (layer of cells where growth in diameter occurs) builds tissues — wood inside and bark outside.

Outer bark protects tree from injuries.

Heartwood

Inner bark

Roots

The buds, root tips, and cambium layer are the growing parts. The tree takes in oxygen over its entire surface through breathing pores on leaves, twigs, branches, trunk, and roots.

Taproot

Task 6: Suggesting Modifications to a Visual

Look at the visual. What, if anything, would you modify? Observe the numbering in the visual. How has the speaker ordered the discussion of the bone?

Bone: structure

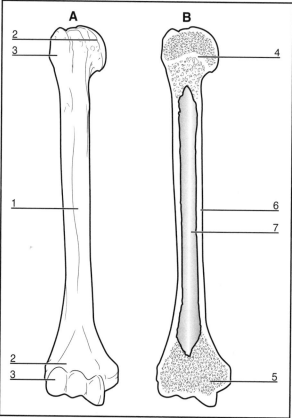

A Long bone (the humerus)
B Section through a long bone

1 Shaft (diaphysis)
2 End (epiphysis)
3 Articular cartilage
4 Epiphyseal line
5 Cancellous (spongy) bone containing
   red marrow
6 Compact bone
7 Medullary cavity containing yellow
   marrow

Tips for Enhancing Your Visual

> ❯ Make your visual attractive but simple.

> ❯ Make your image large and eye-catching. Add color. Make all lettering clear and large enough to read.

> ❯ Remove all extraneous wording from your visual, including the names of parts you don't plan to discuss.

> ❯ Provide a title.

> ❯ Label all major parts or components.

> ❯ Include the source from which the visual was taken.

A Back-Up Plan for Mechanical Failures

If you are worried that your projection equipment might break down or will be unavailable, prepare one of these options.

- Show the visual from your laptop. Put the laptop on a desk or tall cart and ask students to move so that they can see it.

- Put your visual on handouts for the class. If you use handouts, however, you may lose eye contact with the audience and may not be able to gesture effectively.

- If you have access to a television, you may be able to project your visual onto the TV.

- If you have access to an overhead projector, make a back-up transparency using a photocopier or copy service.

- Bring the visual on a piece of paper and project it using an opaque projector or tape it to the wall or blackboard.

- If your object is easy to draw, use the blackboard or whiteboard. Draw the object and label the parts quickly as you go through your speech or draw the object before your speech so that you can make the best use of your time allotment.

Task 7: Describing a Tire

In this speech, the speaker has chosen to talk about a simple object that people may not give much thought to. While most people can easily recognize a tire, they may not know the various parts of a tire and what their function is.

Working with a partner or in a small group, read this speech aloud. Then answer the questions on page 46.

What Is a Tire?

Most people drive a car without giving much thought to their tires. But tires are an important safety feature of a vehicle. And they also give you a comfortable ride. We tend to think of a tire as one big piece of black rubber that's shaped like a hollow donut. But tires are actually made up of several important parts.

(*Points to Visual 1*) The part that makes contact with the road is called the tread. Treads are made of different types of rubber. They provide traction for the car and also help cushion the ride and cut down on noise.

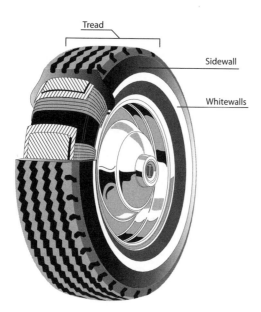

You may have noticed that treads have different kinds of waffle-like patterns. The reason they're different is that they're designed for different types of needs. For example, some tread patterns are made for heavy-duty wear or to send large quantities of water away from the car. Some create more traction in snow.

(*Points to Visual 1*) The part of the tire above the tread is the sidewall. The sidewalls are the sides of the tire. You've probably seen white sidewalls in the movies or on older cars. These are called whitewalls.

Visual 1

(*Points to Visual 2*) Both the treads and sidewalls are reinforced from underneath by a series of plies, which are layers of fabric or metal cords. They give the rubber more stability and keep it from stretching.

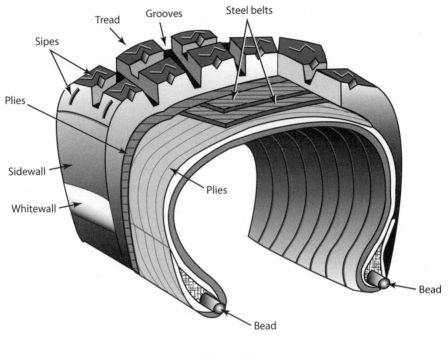

Visual 2

(*Points to Visual 2*) After the sidewalls are the beads. They're the edges of the tire. The beads are made up of thick steel wire that is encased by the plies. They're important because they make it possible to connect the tire to the rim of the wheel. They've been designed to fit tightly to the rim to prevent air from escaping.

Steel belts are plies located below the tread. They give the tire more rigidity to help it make contact with the road. They also give the car a smoother ride and improve the longevity of the tire.

So, those are the main parts of the tire. Now when you go to the store, you'll have a better idea of what you're looking for and you'll be able to ask for tires whose features are designed for your specific needs.

Discussion Questions

1. Who is the audience? How can you tell?

2. The speaker doesn't actually give a definition of a tire? Do you think the speaker should have included it? Why or why not?

3. What words does the speaker define? Were the definitions clear?

4. What organizational strategy does the speaker use? What connecting words does the speaker use to move from one part of the tire to another?

5. If the speaker is allowed one to two more minutes of time to expand the speech, what information would you like the speaker to include? Explain. (Choose 2.) Would the speaker have to include any additional visuals?

   - Do they use natural rubber from trees to make tires?

   - You didn't define *sipes* and *grooves* in the second visual. What are they for?

   - What is a snow tire?

   - How are whitewalls made?

   - How are the plies different from each other?

   - I've heard the expression *steel-belted radial*. What does it mean?

6. Read some comments from the critique of the presentation. What's your opinion of the presentation?

   - I'm a mechanical engineer, so the speech covered some very basic information I already know. But people in the class are from fields like psychology, architecture, and public health, so I think they learned some useful things about tires.

   - I've never driven in snow, so I'd kind of like to see what snow tire treads look like.

   - I liked the speech but would have liked to know more about tire design and production.

Part 2: Comparing Objects

In many academic situations, speakers not only describe objects but also compare them to other related objects in order to highlight similarities and differences. For example, a presenter may compare the structure of a suspension bridge to that of a cable-stayed bridge, a deciduous tree to an evergreen, an older type of wind turbine to a newer one, or a kitchen in one country to one in another country.

Rather than simply describing differences, the speaker may also offer a critique of the two objects, outlining the pros and cons of each object. In Part 2 of this unit, the focus will be on highlighting similarities and differences. Critiquing will be discussed later in the text.

Task 8: Preparing for a Comparison-Contrast Speech

Imagine that you are going to give a talk comparing and contrasting butterflies and moths. You've listed some information that highlights important characteristics of both. Now you need to order the information on page 48 in a logical way. Working in groups, talk about what organizational strategy (strategies) you would use to present the characteristics. Which way does your group prefer? Why? Number the boxes in the order you think the information should appear. Then answer the questions on pages 48–49.

Butterflies	Moths
Insects (exoskeleton or outer skeleton)	Insects (exoskeleton or outer skeleton)
Front and hind wing	Front and hind wing
Wings have scales of different colors	Wings have scales of different colors
Body has scales	Body has thick coat of scales, looks furry and plump
Active during the day	Some active during the day, generally active beginning at dusk
Most have two antennae with knobs at the end	Two tapered or branched antennae
Divided into three parts: head, thorax, abdomen	Divided into three parts: head, thorax, abdomen
Drink nectar and other liquids from proboscis (tube-like structure); roll up proboscis when not using it	Drink nectar and other liquids from proboscis (tube-like structure); roll up proboscis when not using it
Use antennae for flying; smell with antennae	Use antennae for flying; smell with antennae
Butterfly wings generally face upwards when at rest	Moth wings usually parallel to ground when at rest
Taste with their feet	Taste with their feet

—Discussion Questions—————————————————

1. Which strategy (strategies) listed on page 33 (general to specific, spatially, from the most important to the least important or vice versa, logically) did your group decide to use? Was there general agreement in your group about the best way to organize the information? Did you use any strategies that weren't in the list?

2. What devices does this speaker use to discuss similarities and differences?

- Both butterflies and moths are insects. All insects have an exoskeleton. And like other insects, butterflies and moths are divided into three parts: the head, thorax, and abdomen.

- Butterflies are active during the day. You can also see some moths during the day but they're generally active at dusk.

- Butterfly antennae have knobs at the ends of their antennae. In contrast, moths have branches so their antennae look feathered or tapered.

- A difference that can be useful in distinguishing butterflies and moths is that butterfly wings usually face upwards when they're resting, whereas moth wings are usually parallel to the ground.

- Moths look furrier and plumper than butterflies because they have a thin coat of scales on their bodies.

What other devices could the speaker have used?

3. In this speech, what terms need to be defined? Why don't definitions play a large role in this speech?

4. How could you define the term *proboscis* using a three-part formal definition structure

Term + class + Essential differences/distinguishing characteristics

Term → _____

Class → _____

Essential differences/distinguishing characteristics → _____

_____

5. This paragraph* contrasts two fish, the largemouth bass and the smallmouth bass. Underline the devices that the speaker uses to distinguish these two fish.

In the largemouth bass, the dorsal fins are deeply notched, whereas in the smallmouth the notch between the two parts of the dorsal fin is less deeply notched. The largemouth bass is gonna fight a lot harder pound for pound but I think the smallmouth fights a lot faster pound for pound.

*Text from MICASE, modified.

Task 9: Using PowerPoint Slides

When projecting a single picture, it may not be necessary to use PowerPoint. It might be simpler to project a file from your computer or flash drive. However, when comparing two objects, you may feel like you would like to highlight similarities and differences using several slides. For example, when comparing butterflies and moths, you could use

- side-by side pictures of a butterfly and a moth
- close-up pictures of the antennae of both the butterfly and the moth

1. What other slides would you recommend for this speech?
2. What option would you use if you found out at the last minute that the computer projector was broken?

Maintaining Contact with the Audience

Checking for Understanding

When you give a presentation, some members of the audience may have problems understanding you. For example, if you mispronounce key vocabulary words, speak too softly or quickly, or choose a topic that is too technical, you may "lose your audience." Pause during your speech to make sure your audience members are following you by checking for understanding. Here are some expressions used in actual academic settings to check for understanding.*

1. Everybody understand?**
2. Does everybody understand . . . ?
3. So did everyone understand that?***
4. You understand?
5. You understand that?
6. Is that clear? Is that okay?
7. Is that clear? No? Yes?
8. Are you following here?***
9. Everyone understand?
10. You following?
11. Is this clear?
12. Are you with me?

---

*Examples 1–10 are taken from MICASE.
**Notice that the speaker has omitted the auxiliary here and in Expressions 4, 5, 9, and 10.
****That* and *here* likely refer to something the speaker has just said.

Pronunciation

Stress

As discussed in Unit 1, improper pausing places extra demands on listeners and may make a presentation seem choppy and hesitant. Another pronunciation problem that can interfere with listeners' comprehension is improper stress or emphasis. In English, words that provide information to the listener, such as nouns, adjectives, verbs, and adverbs, are generally stressed. If these key words are left unstressed, the listener may not hear valuable information. Less important words that carry little information, such as articles *(the, a, an)*, prepositions *(in, at)*, and pronouns *(he, she, it)*, are generally not stressed unless the speaker purposely highlights them.

Speakers who fail to stress words that occur before a pause or at the end of an utterance may find it even more difficult to convey their message because new information often occurs at these two places in English. If listeners can't hear new information, they may lose the speaker's main idea. Look at the sentence from the introduction of an object speech.

> *This musical instrument is called a harp.*

There are several key words in this utterance, including *musical* and *instrument*. However, *harp* is probably the most important word in the sentence. The speaker is introducing the harp as the topic of his speech. If a key word isn't stressed and, consequently, the listeners don't hear it, they will have to rely on their eyes (i.e., viewing a picture or the object itself) and contextual cues.

How does stress help the listener? When speakers stress a word, they speak louder. As a result, the word takes longer to say. This makes it easier for the listener to hear it. Unstressed words, on the other hand, are said more quickly.

What does the speaker actually stress? If the word has only one syllable, such as *harp*, the whole word is stressed.

> *This is a HARP.*

If the word has two syllables, such as *guitar*, one syllable is generally stressed and the other unstressed. In the case of *guitar*, the second syllable is stressed.

> *This is a gui/TAR.*

However, sometimes both syllables are stressed, one with heavier, or primary, stress (´) and the other with lighter, or secondary, stress (`), as in *trombone*.

> *This is a* TRÒM/ *BÓNE.*

In words with three syllables, two syllables will also be stressed, one with primary stress (´) and the other with secondary stress (ˋ). One example is the word *violin*. Here secondary stress occurs on the first syllable and primary stress on the last syllable. But the middle syllable is unstressed (˘).

> *This is a vì/ŏ/LÍN.*

How does a speaker know which syllables to stress? If you look in a good English-English dictionary, the stressed syllables of all words are marked (except words with only one syllable). Alternative pronunciations are also listed. Word stress may vary with different dialects of English; this can initially cause comprehension problems for listeners.

Task 10: Word Stress

Read the short speech on an important object from the speaker's country. Mark the words in each utterance that you think the speaker should stress. Use [´] to indicate what syllable should be stressed. Then underline the word in each utterance that should be stressed the most. Generally, this word will occur toward the end of a pause. Suggestions for pauses are indicated with // where the speaker is likely to slow down and /// where the speaker is likely to stop.

Keep in mind that words that carry meaning are generally stressed. Words that are stressed the most often occur at the end of a natural pause.

Hi.// I'm Marie from Canada./// One important object in my country//

is the recycling bin./// It's simple. /// It only has two parts:// a large

container and a top. /// We can put paper, plastic, and metal in our

recycling bin./// These things can be reused to make new products,//

maybe even new recycling bins.///

Review the paragraph from Unit 1. The pauses are clearly marked but stress isn't. What words might the speaker stress? Of these words, which words will the speaker most likely stress the most?

Now, // John's studying business // at the University of Michigan. ///

His major area of interest // is managing nonprofit corporations. ///

Before John went to college, // he traveled around the world for two

years. ///

Task 11: Emphasizing Keywords in a Short Talk

Choose an object from daily life in your country to create a very short talk of five or six utterances using the outline. Practice emphasizing key words and de-emphasizing less important words that do not provide important information to the listener. Practice your talk with a partner. Ask your partner for feedback. Where did you need to stress a word more clearly? Then repeat the talk to your partner or a larger audience.

Hi, my name's _____ and I'm from _____. One

important object in my country is _____. It's

used to _____. _____

usually has _____ main parts: _____. The

_____ is used to _____. The

_____ is for _____.

Task 12: Evaluating Your Use of Stress

Record the talk you gave in Task 11 and write four sentences from it. Underline each word that you stressed and indicate which syllable(s) of the word you stressed the loudest ('). Did you stress too many or too few words? Make corrections and practice saying those sentences again.

Task 13: Object Presentation

Prepare a four- or five-minute presentation on an object(s) from your field of study. Choose one of these options:

- describe an object
- describe an object and then briefly point out how it differs from another object
- compare and contrast two objects, giving each equal time
- give a tour of an object (see Task 14 on page 56)

Consider choosing a topic that the audience members are familiar with but does not know much about. If your area focuses on abstract concepts, you may wish to describe a standard written text commonly used in your field, such as a contract, lab report, case study, evaluation form, pharmaceutical insert, or stock report; or a physical space, such as a courtroom or historical sight. (See Task 14 on page 56.)

Do not discuss a process or problem plus solution for this speech. These speech types will be discussed later in the textbook. If you are in doubt about your topic, discuss it with your instructor.

1. Keep your time limit in mind. Decide what information you want to include in your presentation. Focus on the major parts of your object(s) and eliminate the others.
2. Place your object(s) in a larger context and give adequate background information.
3. Choose an organizational pattern (or patterns) that suits your topic.

4. Think about the connecting devices you will use to point to parts of your object(s) and move from one part to the next. If you are contrasting two objects, use devices that signal similarities (such as *both*, *likewise*, and *similar*) and differences (such as *but*, *however*, *in contrast*, and *on the other hand*).

5. Consider using an organizational indicator statement.

6. Make the PowerPoint slides you will need for your presentation. Make sure that (1) you include necessary titles and labels, (2) your pictures and lettering are clear, (3) all unnecessary writing is eliminated, and (4) you include your source. Be prepared to use the blackboard or other visual tools if you don't plan to use slides. Making fancy visuals can be time-consuming. Be sure you leave enough time to devote to your speech.

7. Practice your speech three or four times by reading out loud and standing. The last time, record it. Listen to your speech and decide what sections need improvement. Use the evaluation form on pages 57–58 as a guide. Then practice several more times. Critique your non-verbal behavior, too.

8. Before you give your speech, decide where you will stop to make sure that the audience is following you. Rely on the expressions in Checking for Understanding on page 50 to help you.

Giving a Tour

Another way to approach your object presentation is by designing a tour. If you have chosen a space or area to describe, you may want to give the audience a tour of the object by walking through it. Your job as tour guide will be to explain the various parts of the object as you move along.

Some objects that lend themselves to this approach include

- ❐ a submarine
- ❐ a Japanese or other traditional home
- ❐ an apartment or other structure with devices for a handicapped person
- ❐ a laboratory in your area of studies
- ❐ a historic battlefield
- ❐ a public garden
- ❐ a dental office

❑ a commercial or historic kitchen
❑ a courtroom
❑ the library room
❑ a cave
❑ an ancient temple site

Task 14: Preparing Your Tour Speech

Choose a location to give a tour of and answer the questions.

1. What will you say to your tour group before beginning the tour? What background information will you provide?

2. Where will you start the tour?

3. How will you organize the tour? Spatially? From more to less important parts? Logically? Using more than one organizational pattern?

4. What parts of the tour will you highlight? What information will you provide about the function/functions of those parts?

5. What expressions will you use to explain the location of a particular area and its relationship to other areas:

Here are some examples. Add more to the list.

> *As we turn right, you'll notice*
>
> *Now look straight ahead*
>
> *To the left of X is*
>
> *Over in the corner next to the X and Y is*
>
> *Directly in back of X is*
>
> *If you look up, you can see*
>
> *Be careful not to bump your head on the*
>
> *There is usually an X in the middle of this room*

Review useful information on organization, pointing, non-verbal behavior, definitions, etc., to help you design and give your presentation.

Object Speech Evaluation

Listen to your final speech. Then, complete the Object Speech Evaluation Form. Be sure to provide specific comments in the Comments section. Also, set goals for your next speech.

If you prefer to evaluate your speech with one or two partners, discuss your strengths and weaknesses and then complete the evaluation form. If you wish, include feedback from your partners on the form.

Object Speech Evaluation Form Name: _____				
	(Make a check in the appropriate column)			
	Good	OK	Needs Work	Comments (include specific problems you noticed)
Topic Interesting? Appropriate for the audience?				
Introduction Placed object(s) in a larger context? Defined the object(s)? Included the purpose or importance of the object(s)?				
Organization Chose an effective organizational strategy/strategies? Used organization indicator statement(s)? Used connecting devices effectively?				
Pointing words and spatial connectors suitable for Introducing the object? Pointing out its parts? Moving on to a subsequent part? Relating the parts to each other?				
Purpose Clearly explained the purpose or function of all the labeled parts?				
Comparison and contrast Pointed out major similarities and differences between the objects and their parts. Effectively used devices for comparison and contrast.				

	(Make a check in the appropriate column)			
	Good	OK	Needs Work	Comments (include specific problems you noticed)
Gestures Hands were free to point at the visual(s)? Gestures were expressive?				
Conclusion Smooth? Reiterated the importance of the object?				
Visual(s) Large and clear? Properly labeled? Unnecessary writing eliminated? Source included?				
Pace Not too fast or too slow? Smooth rather than hesitant, choppy?				
Interaction with audience Friendly, approachable speaker? Good eye contact (looked at all the listeners)? Checked to see if listeners were understanding? Strong, confident voice?				

Pronunciation

(specific problems)

Other comments

Goals for my next presentation (list 2–3 areas that you want to improve for your next presentation)

Unit 3 —————————————————————

Explaining a Process or Procedure

Members of all academic disciplines work with processes or procedures. Students and faculty explain, discover, create, implement, modify, and follow processes or procedures as part of their training or professional responsibilities. *Processes* are generally viewed as a progression or series of events, steps, or changes that have a beginning and end or end result. However, some processes are cyclical or continuing. Processes can be natural or can involve human intervention. Established processes for performing specific tasks are generally referred to as *procedures*.

Speeches about processes can be organized in various ways, depending on the purpose of the speech. For example, if speakers want to highlight several recent improvements on a process, they may simply enumerate the modifications using listing as the main organizational strategy. However, if their purpose is to explain a process, they will generally focus on its steps and will choose chronological order as their main organizational strategy. In this unit, chronological order will be emphasized.

In academic English, it can be more challenging to explain a process than to describe a single object. Both natural processes that take place without human intervention and procedures that primarily involve the interaction of people with tools, machines, and materials can be complex. Topics such as how soil is formed, concrete is made, pollutants are removed from the soil, a film is edited, a legal case goes through the court system, or a corporation is developed may include a number of events. Therefore, presenters need to plan their speeches carefully. For example, they have to decide what background information the audience needs to know before presenting the process, what terms may be unfamiliar to the audience and when to introduce and explain them, and what strategies for presenting each step in the process will enhance listeners' comprehension.

For your next presentation, you will explain a process or procedure from your field of studies. Since you will likely be speaking to a general academic audience and will have time constraints, your presentation can be neither too simple nor too long and complex. Make a list of several processes related to your field. As you go through the exercises in this unit, evaluate these processes as possible final presentation topics.

Task 1: Evaluating a Visual

Look at the information in this simple visual that is based on a student drawing. What procedure has the speaker chosen to discuss? Then answer the questions on this page and page 61.

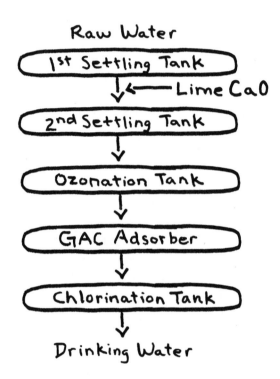

Discussion Questions

1. What is the topic of this process speech? Do you think it is appropriate for a general academic audience? Would you personally be interested in listening to this speech? What might it depend on?

2. Approximately how many steps does the speaker discuss? How can you tell? Which organization indicator statement (see Unit 1, page 8, and Unit 2, page 40) could the speaker use to introduce the steps?

3. What is the only information the speaker includes in the visual? Do you think it's enough?

4. What are some of the terms that the speaker will likely define during the speech? Is the speaker more likely to explain these terms in the introduction or when explaining the process?

5. Compare the speaker's visual with this second one. What are the main advantages to each? Think about which one would:

- take less time to make
- be more likely to attract the audience's attention
- keep the audience's attention on the speaker
- provide a more in-depth discussion of the water treatment cycle
- give the presenter more time to practice the speech
- help the audience if the speaker has some trouble pronouncing some terms
- allow the speaker to reveal information only one step at a time

The Water Treatment Cycle

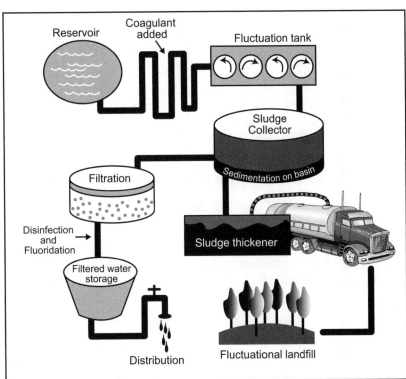

6. Using PowerPoint, how would you design a visual or series of visuals for this presentation? How long do you think it would take you?

The topic of this speech seems to be well chosen. It is relevant to a general academic audience because it relates to our daily lives but at the same time may not be familiar to members of the audience. However, if the speech is too simplistic, dry, or complex, then the speaker could lose the attention of the audience. Therefore, the speaker will want to make the speech as informative and interesting as possible without making it too technical.

Both visuals focus on the location in which each step in the water treatment process takes place. The first speaker's visual is neat and clearly labeled but not very eye-catching. However, it likely took presenter only a few minutes to make, allowing more time for practice. In addition, the visual doesn't reveal much information, which means that the audience will tend to focus on what the speaker is saying rather than the visual itself.

The second visual is much more attractive and provides more in-depth information about the process. This could also be a disadvantage because the audience may initially spend time scanning the visual rather than focusing on the speaker. One solution to this would be to design a series of PowerPoint slides, each showing a phase in the process, or to use one slide that reveals the steps, one by one, as the speaker moves through the process.

With either visual, the speaker will need to define terminology, such as *settling tank*, *ozonation tank*, *flocculation tank*, and *sludge*. These are best explained during the step in the process in which they are introduced.

Introductions to Process Speeches

1. Using Rhetorical Questions

One way to begin a process speech is to use a rhetorical question. Rhetorical questions are questions that the speaker poses to the audience but that don't require an answer. Rhetorical questions are an effective means of opening a speech for several reasons.

- ❑ Rhetorical questions are more apt to get the audience's attention than an opener like *Today I'm going to talk about . . . .*
- ❑ Rhetorical questions gradually lead the audience into the topic of the speech, and thus may more effectively guarantee that the audience is following the speaker.
- ❑ By using rhetorical questions, the speaker begins a relationship with the audience that can be maintained throughout the speech.

One drawback to using rhetorical questions is that the audience may think that some questions are real and that the speaker is asking the audience to answer them. One way speakers solve this problem is by not pausing long enough for the audience to respond.

Task 2: Identifying Rhetorical Questions

Look at the introduction and identify any rhetorical questions. In which sentence does the speaker introduce the topic?

① Have you ever thought about where the water you drink comes from? ② Many times it comes from rivers and lakes that have contaminated water. ③ How is this water purified so that it is safe for you to drink? ④ Today, I'm going to explain a process commonly used to purify drinking water called the water treatment cycle.

2. Providing Background Information

Another way to begin is using background information. Before going too far into an explanation of the process, the speaker usually needs to give necessary background information. The introduction may include

- ❑ the definition of the process
- ❑ the purpose of the process (if it is not included in the definition)
- ❑ other important definitions
- ❑ equipment and/or material used in the process
- ❑ the people involved in the process
- ❑ the number of steps in the process

Task 3: Providing Background Information

Read the introduction to a presentation on the Rankine cycle. Then, working with a partner, place a check mark (✔) before the types of background information the speaker used.

_____ 1. A definition of the process

_____ 2. The purpose(s) of the process

_____ 3. Other important definitions or explanation of terms

_____ 4. Equipment and/or material used in the process

_____ 5. People involved in the process

_____ 6. The number of steps in the process

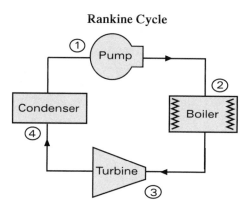

Rankine Cycle

Rankine Cycle

① Good morning, everyone.

② Today, I'd like to talk about a basic thermal cycle usually used in a power plant. It is called Rankine cycle.

③ Before I launch into an introduction of the Rankine cycle, I would like to explain what a thermal cycle means first. Simply speaking, a thermal cycle is a cycle that is related to some thermodynamic property change, such as temperature, pressure, or density.

④ Okay, now let's go back to the Rankine cycle. Basically the cycle is composed of four steps, as you can see in the figure. The working fluid usually used is water. And the working fluid here experiences all the steps inside the cycle.

In the introduction, the speaker successfully (1) introduces the process that he is going to describe (the Rankine cycle) and defines it, (2) explains terms *(thermal cycle* and *thermodynamic property change)* that the audience may need to understand the process, (3) states the number of steps in the process (four) by using an organization indicator statement, and (4) tells the audience the material used in the process (water).

Task 4: How the Rankine Cycle Works

Finish reading the speech on the Rankine cycle. Then answer the questions on page 66.

⑤ Now let's follow the flow direction of the fluid to see how this cycle works.

⑥ At the beginning, the liquid is pumped into the boiler by a pump, and then inside the boiler the liquid is heated into a vapor.

⑦ In the boiler, the liquid reaches a high temperature and high pressure, which means the energy level is increased. This is also the function of the boiler—to increase the energy level of the working fluid so that the fluid can do work.

⑧ You'll see how this working fluid does the work in the next step. Now let's move to the next step.

⑨ The high-pressure, high-temperature vapor moves to the turbine to drive the generators and generate electricity.

⑩ And after going through this turbine, the working fluid is cooled down, which means the energy level is reduced. Why the energy level is reduced is because some of the energy is used to drive the generator. That means the working fluid is doing some work.

⑪ Okay, then after this step, the cooled vapor travels to a condenser and inside the condenser, the vapor is condensed to a liquid again, so that the cycle can be repeated again and again.

⑫ Now that's my brief introduction to how the Rankine cycle works.

(Presentation by Jr-Hung Tsai, with minor changes.)

──**Discussion Questions**────────────────────

1. What are the four steps in the Rankine cycle?

2. What is the purpose of *let's* in Sections 4, 5, and 8?

3. What time connectors does the speaker use to move from one step to another?

4. What is the purpose of *you* in Section 8?

5. What verb tense does the speaker use to describe the steps in the process?

6. Does the speaker generally use active or passive voice?

Organizing the Process: Connecting Devices

As long as your introduction contains the necessary background information, you should have few problems organizing the main part of the speech, the explanation of the process, because the process mainly involves sequential steps (several single steps that occur one after the other). However, don't overlook the importance of connecting devices to move from one step of your process to another.

The Expression Let's

The expression *Let's* is commonly used by speakers to inform the listeners of a transition to a new topic or subtopic. It's often preceded by *Now, Okay, So,* or *Alright*:

> Now let's move to the next step.
>
> Okay, let's go back to the Rankine cycle.
>
> So, let's practice.

It commonly occurs before verbs like *move on to, look at, see,* or *go back.*

Let's (Let us), by definition, includes the audience. Therefore, using it in your presentation can be one way to enhance your relationship with the audience.

Time Connectors

In Unit 1 you used time connectors in introduction speeches to link sequences of events from past to present. Time connectors such as *at the beginning, first, and then, when you finish,* and *then after this step* are used to explain the chronological relationships between the steps in the process and to inform the audience that the speaker is moving on to the next step of the process. For these reasons, the connectors are generally found at the beginning of the utterance.

Explaining the Process: Tense, Voice, and the Imperative (Command)

Tense

Present tense is generally used to explain a process, especially if the process is a standard procedure or a predictable or recurring event, such as *the liquid is heated, the sediment moves, the sludge is collected.* If, however, a speaker chooses to explain a procedure that has already been specifically carried out (e.g., as part of a research study), then the past tense is useful. In this case, *I, we,* or *they* can generally be used as the subject.

Voice

The speaker generally uses **passive voice** when an action is carried out by "an actor" such as a person, machine, or another outside force. The focus of the speech, however, is not the actor but the process (e.g., the liquid *is pumped,* the water *is collected*). By using passive voice, the speaker is able to place the topic or current focus in subject position, which is customary in English.

If the process itself is viewed as a natural one, **active voice** is commonly used (e.g., when the rain *falls* to the ground, the river *flows* to the ocean). Active voice can also be used to de-emphasize outside intervention (e.g., as the boxes *travel* along the conveyer belt; the boxes *are moved* along the conveyer belt). In this case, the process is treated by the speaker as a natural one. Active voice may have been chosen for its simplicity or economy.

Active voice may also be used to focus on the key participants in an academic procedure. In this case, *I* or *we* could be used. However, if there are several key players in a procedure, the speaker will need to clarify the roles of each.

> The **judge** instructs the jury on what law to apply in the case. The **jury** applies the law and decides the outcome of the case. Both parties have the right to appeal the decision of the jury.

The Imperative (Command)

The imperative or command form is commonly used in a process speech when the speaker wishes to instruct the listeners on how to carry out a task. Giving instructions is far more frequent in some university contexts than others and may take place under more informal circumstances rather than during more formal academic events. Laboratory assistants, art and music instructors, and dental and nursing students may often give instructions as part of their regular interactions with students, colleagues, and clients. In these cases, there may be more interaction between the speaker and the listener(s).

Instead of using the imperative (e.g., *stand*) speakers commonly use *you* + verb (*you stand*). It can be viewed as a statement rather than a command. *You* need not refer to a specific individual or group of individuals but can be used to refer to anyone carrying out a process.

The chart on page 69 outlines passive and active voice and the imperative.

Passive Voice	Active Voice	Imperative (Command)
The process is generally carried out by a person, machine, or another outside force (outside intervention).	1. The process is viewed as a natural one. 2. The speaker wishes to de-emphasize inter-vention by an outside force. 3. There are several key players in the process, each with important roles.	The speaker gives instruct-ions for the audience to follow.
Examples: *After the first step is complete, lime is added to the water.* *Finally, the rocket is drawn to earth by gravity.* Notice that *lime* and *rocket* are in the subject position because they are the topic or speaker's current focus. New information follows. (Compare this with *Finally gravity draws the rocket to earth,* which would change the topic/focus from *rocket* to *gravity*.)	Examples: *Acid rain falls on the soil. . . .* *The water flows from the first tank to the second. (Cf. The water is pumped from the first tank to the second.)* *The judge chooses the instructions, but the jury applies them to the case at hand.*	Examples: *Repeat this step.* *Collect the liquid in a sterile container.* *Compare these two advertising strategies.*

Look at the Rankine Cycle speech again. Do you think the speaker meant to say the working fluid is *cooled down* (passive voice), which would indicate that there was an outside force? Or do you think the speaker views the process as a natural one and meant to use active voice instead (*the working fluid cools down*)?

Observe how the speaker uses the imperative in Task 5 on pages 70–71.

Giving an Instructions Speech

Some procedures lend themselves to being explained by means of a chronologically ordered set of instructions. The topic of the following instructions speech, given by a nursing student, is how to help someone who is choking.

Task 5: An Instructions Speech

Read the script aloud with a group or partner. As you read, think about the strategies she uses and how she develops her introduction. Then answer the questions on page 72.

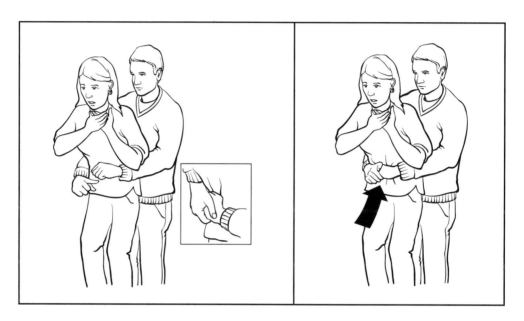

How to Help Someone Who Is Choking

① Hello, everybody. If one of our classmates started choking seriously within the next few minutes, ask yourself—would you be able to help him or her? And how would you help him or her?

② I think you know that most emergencies happen, uh, in or near the home, so you are more likely to give care to a family member or a friend than someone you don't know. So knowing how to rescue people from choking is worthwhile. And so today I am going to tell you how to help people who are choking.

③ Choking is a serious breathing emergency. A person who's choking has his or her airway blocked by food or another object. The airway can be partially blocked or can be completely blocked. A person who has a partially blocked airway can breathe in enough air to cough or even speak.

④ So if you see that the victim is coughing forcefully, what you should do is to encourage him or her to cough up the object. However, if a person's airway becomes completely blocked, the person can't cough forcefully, speak, or breathe. So what you must do is immediately give a series of quick hard thrusts to the victim's abdomen so that the air in the lungs will push the object out of the airway. Before I move on to the steps for giving abdominal thrusts, any questions?

⑤ Okay, so let's go on to the steps for giving abdominal thrusts. This is a conscious person and you can see the person is choking. [*Speaker makes choking noises.*] First, you stand behind the victim and put your arms around the victim's waist. Make a fist with one hand and put the thumb side of the fist here in the victim's abdomen right above the navel but under the rib cage. [*Demonstrates while she is speaking.*] That's clear?

⑥ And then the second step. Put your other hand on your fist and make quick, inward and upward thrusts into the abdomen, like this. [*Demonstrates while she is speaking.*] And, uh, you have to repeat this until the victim coughs up the object.

⑦ So you can do it by yourself right now. So let's practice it because I think this is helpful. Just just place your fist about the navel and below the rib cage. And then grab your fist and make an inward and upward movement. [*Demonstrates.*] You can feel the pressure. Don't make it forcefully.

⑧ So, any questions about this procedure? Okay.

[*The speaker goes on to discuss what to do if the victim is unconscious.*]

(Speech by Tassanee Prasopkittikun, with slight modifications.)

Discussion Questions

1. How does the speaker open the speech?

2. What background information does she provide before explaining the steps in the process?

3. Where does the speaker begin discussing the first step?

4. What linking words does the speaker use in her speech, especially to move from one step to another?

5. What tense does the speaker use to explain the steps?

6. The speaker doesn't use passive voice to discuss the steps. What does the speaker use instead and why?

7. Why does the speaker use the modal *have to* at the end of Section 6 before having the audience try the step on themselves?

8. How does the speaker keep in touch with the audience?

9. Does the speaker need visuals for this speech? Explain.

Using Modals in Process Speeches

When you are giving your process speech, you may find yourself using modals such as

must	*will*
have to	*can*
should	*would (hypothetical)*

Modals are often unnecessary in process speeches if the speaker's goal is to explain rather than to instruct, train, admonish, or warn. If the steps in the process are generally repeatable, predictable, standard, or intrinsic to the process, you can likely reduce the use of modals to streamline your explanation. However, if modals in some way clarify or enhance your explanation, you may wish to include them.

Task 6: Modal Use

Read the steps. Decide if the modal serves a useful purpose or if it could be eliminated. Is your decision based on audience? The purpose of the presentation? If it were eliminated, what would the speaker say?

1. The liquid has to be stirred for at least three minutes.

2. During the initial stage, the goals of the revitalization project should be clarified. After that, information about potential sites can be collected.

3. The building plan must be approved by the housing council before work begins.

4. After finishing this procedure, you'll clean the area with disinfectant.

5. First you would anesthetize the area and then you'd make a small incision with a scalpel.

Task 7: Subject, Tense, and Voice

With a partner, read the five excerpts from the Michigan Corpus of Academic Spoken English (MICASE). Each excerpt describes a process. The verbs used to describe the process are in bold. Does the speaker use passive voice, active voice, the imperative, *you* or *we* + verb, or a modal? Explain why. What tense does the speaker use? Are the speakers consistent?

1. BIOLOGY OF FISHES GROUP ACTIVITY

What we normally do is you **go out** and you would **catch** a bunch of fish and you would **mark** them. You **mark** them in a number of ways. One way is to clip the fin. You **take** the clip out and then you **put** the fish back . . . .

2. PROFESSIONAL MECHANICAL ENGINEERING SEMINAR

The next thing we did was we **formed** that film under the step-load kind of test, and when the film was nice and dark and uniform, we then **dried off** that surface with solvent.

3. OCEANOGRAPHY LECTURE

To carry sediment out into the ocean very far, if you think about it, what happens? The, the rivers **flow down** to the ocean right? In general in most places not every place but in most places, as the river **comes down** from the mountains down through the hills down through the coastal plain, the level or the steepness of the slope of the river **gets** lower and lower, and then when the river **hits** the ocean, in a way it's like hitting a s— a rock wall. I mean that it can't go any deeper than that, and so the flow **stops**, in terms of river flow. And other processes take over. Currents, tidal flushing in and out, longshore currents, wave generated currents, things like that, **will** then **take** that sediment that's delivered by the rivers, and **move** it around a little bit.

4. OFFICE HOUR DISCUSSION IN STATISTICS

You're gonna **calculate**, or you already have calculated X-bar and Y-bar, but you wanna now see whether difference in the sample means is significantly different from ten, okay? Significantly higher than ten so you're gonna **subtract** off ten instead of subtracting off zero. And then still **divide** by that standard error. That's your test statistic now. And you just **do** the test the same way you would with any other two observed test statistics.

5. INORGANIC CHEMISTRY

I **put** sodium nitrate one drop here and then in the next little grid and so on. And then you're gonna **take** a dropping pipette and you're going to **add** the anion. And you're going to just **mix** two drops together . . . .*

---

*All five excerpts (pages 73–74) appear with minor modifications.

Task 8: A Cylindrical Process

Read the excerpt on predators, animals that prey on or hunt smaller animals. Then answer the questions.

1. Does the speaker use active or passive voice?

2. What connecting devices and modals are used?

3. How does the speaker indicate that this is a cyclical process?

4. How does the speaker show cause and effect?

GENERAL ECOLOGY LECTURE

We have a high prey population, and the predators then eat a lot and they're doing really well so they reach a very high level. But then, as they eat up the prey, the prey start declining. And then the predators can't get as much food, and they start declining through lower birth rates or higher death rates. And then when the predators get rare, the prey can start increasing again.*

*Excerpt from MICASE, with minor modifications.

Examples of Cleft Sentences Using *What*

Review the sentences from Section 4 of the speech How to Help Someone Who Is Choking.

> *So if you see that the victim is coughing forcefully, what you should do is to encourage him or her to cough up the object.*

> *So what you must do is immediately give a series of quick hard thrusts to the victim's abdomen.*

Notice that the speaker used what is called a cleft sentence using *what*. The speaker may have used this construction as a means of highlighting or giving additional focus to important information or instructions that follow. A *wh*-clause begins the sentence or clause and is generally followed by *is* or another form of *to be*, such as *What I forgot to mention is . . .*, or *What I did was . . . .*

The basic structure of a cleft sentence using *what* is

- **what + subject + (modal) verb +** *is* OR
  + to (optional) + Verb

  What you (must) do immediately is begin CPR.

- **+ gerund**

  What you may prefer is working in small groups.

- **+ noun**

  What this technique is generally known for is its accuracy.

Task 9: Making Cleft Sentences

How can you make cleft sentences from these sentences?

> EXAMPLE 1
>
> *In order to stop the bleeding, you wrap a tourniquet around the person's leg.*
>
> *In order to stop the bleeding, what* + subject + (modal) verb + *is....*
>
> *In order to stop the bleeding what you must do is wrap the tourniquet around the person's leg.*

> EXAMPLE 2
>
> *Today I'll talk about a problem you might have experienced with your cell phone.*
>
> *Today* + *what* + subject + *(will)* verb + *is ....*
>
> *Today what I'll talk about is a problem you may have experienced....*

> EXAMPLE 3
>
> *You'll give five different presentations over the course.*
>
> *What* + subject + *(will)* verb + *is....*
>
> *What you'll do is (to) give five presentations over the course.*

Notice the verb *do* is used here and in Example 1 followed by instructions or responsibilities.

> EXAMPLE 4
>
> *First, the raw water goes to a settling tank.*
>
> *What happens first is (that) the water goes to the settling tank. (c.f. What the operator does first is to direct the flow of water to the settling tank.)*

Notice that the verb *happens* is used when there is no agent performing the task.

How can you make cleft sentences from these sentences?

1. First, I put one drop of sodium nitrate here.

    _____

2. Now, I'm going to show you how the Rankine cycle works.

    _____

3. Normally we go out and catch a bunch of fish.

    _____

4. Today, you're gonna calculate the distance between the moon and the earth.

    _____

5. Finally, I'll discuss how plausible each of these solutions is.

    _____

6. When the river hits the ocean, the flow stops. (Hint: Use *happens.*)

    _____

Gestures

As discussed in Unit 1, novice speakers may (1) fail to use hand gestures or (2) use distracting hand movements during their speeches. Which of the following have you observed yourself doing in your first several presentations?

_____ Grasping your hands behind your back

_____ Grasping your hands in front of you

_____ Keeping your hands in your pockets

_____ Holding something in your hand that kept you from gesturing

_____ Keeping your hands at your sides

_____ Moving your hands in and out of your pocket

_____ Making other hand movements that distracted from your speech, such as scratching your arm or touching your hair

_____ Repeating the same gesture over and over

_____ _____

_____ _____

How have your gestures improved? Under what circumstances do you use gestures more effectively, such as when you feel more comfortable with the contents of your speech.

_____

_____

_____

What gesturing problems do you think you still have?

_____

_____

_____

Tips for Improving Hand Gestures

> ❯ Use rhythmic, beat-like gestures to emphasize key information.

> ❯ Mimick or demonstrate an action, such as pouring liquid or scraping the surface of an object.

> ❯ Describe the object or part of the object that you are discussing by outlining its shape or indicating its size.

> ❯ Demonstrate a property of an object, such as showing that an object bends easily.

> ❯ Use your hand or fingers to point, for example, to a person or a step in a process shown on a visual.

> ❯ Use your fingers to count.*

Task 10: Gesturing

Working in a small group, demonstrate how you would use your hands when saying these sentences during a speech. Share your gestures with other groups and also ask your instructor to demonstrate the gestures he or she might use. Discuss some of the cultural differences and similarities you observed.

1. Today I'd like to introduce you to Said Al-Salem.
2. Pong studied in Britain twice–in 1993 and again in 1997.
3. A camera has an aperture or hole where light passes through.
4. Karin, how is water purified?
5. First, make a fist with your hand.
6. I'm going to describe a receipt from top to bottom.
7. So, there are two steps you need to pay attention to.
8. To the west of my city, there are very tall mountains and to the east it's flat.
9. The water in the machine is then agitated.
10. Gopher turtles live in holes or burrows underground. The entrance to the burrow is shaped like a half moon. It's flat on the bottom and round on the top.
11. This step in the process is very, very dangerous. It has to be done slowly.
12. The process has become simpler, cheaper, and safer.

---

*In English, speakers generally begin counting with their index finger and end with their thumb.

Task 11: Observing the Gestures of Good Speakers

Choose two good speakers, such as a professor and a colleague, and observe their gestures. How effectively do they use their hands? Which of the gestures listed on page 80 did they use? Did they use any of the distracting gestures listed on page 79? Which gestures would you like to incorporate into your speech giving?

Task 12: Evaluating Your Gestures

View the recording of your last speech with the volume off. Watch your hands. What do you do with them? Do you use a lot of gestures? Do you use a variety of gestures to enhance your presentation or do you tend to repeat the same gestures? In what ways do your gestures make your speech more effective? What improvements can you make?

Tips for Using Computer Projection and the Blackboard (or Whiteboard)

Computer Projection

❯ Check all the equipment you need before you begin your presentation. Find out how to get technical assistance in case something goes wrong. Ask what other options, such as a computer monitor or TV, are available.

❯ When using a projection device, adjust the lighting in the room before you start your presentation. Make sure that light from the projection device is not shining in your eyes.

❯ If your projection device is noisy and you don't have access to a different one, be sure to talk loud enough so that everyone in the audience can hear you.

❯ When giving your presentation, talk to the audience, not to the screen or your computer. If possible, stand away from your projection device and keep your back to the screen. Make sure you and the members of the audience can see each other.

❯ If you have trouble gesturing naturally, stand near the screen because then you are in a good position use your hands to point to particular sections of your visual.

Blackboard (or Whiteboard)

❯ If you have to write a lot of information on the blackboard during your speech, your audience will lose interest and you will use up your time allotment. You may also appear unprepared. Use a slide instead. Write the information on the board before the presentation.

❯ A board can be beneficial for writing key terms, giving short explanations, or drawing simple illustrations. Plan how you will use the board before your speech. During your speech, write clearly and quickly.

❯ Before you begin writing, make sure that the board is completely erased.

❯ Chalk or a whiteboard pen can squeak if you hold it incorrectly. To avoid this, slant the chalk (or pen) when you write and hold it lightly.

❯ Stand to the side of information on the board, not in front of it. Talk to the audience, not to the board. Even when writing, try to keep your back against the board as much as possible.

❯ If you are right-handed, stand so that you can write toward yourself rather than away from yourself. If you are left-handed, do the opposite.

Maintaining Contact with the Audience

Checking for Understanding

As discussed in Unit 2, some audience members may have trouble understanding your presentation—for example, when you speak too softly, mispronounce key vocabulary, or choose a topic that is too technical. It's important to check for understanding.

In your last speech, how many times did you check in with your audience? Which of these expressions or variations did you use? If you didn't check for understanding, were you able to tell that the listeners were following you? Explain.

_____ 1. *Everybody understand?*

_____ 2. *Does everybody understand this . . . ?*

_____ 3. *So did everyone understand that?*

_____ 4. *You understand?*

_____ 5. *You understand that?*

_____ 6. *Is that clear? Is that okay?*

_____ 7. *Is that clear? No? Yes?*

_____ 8. *Are you following here?*

_____ 9. *You following?**

_____10. *Is this clear?*

_____11. *Are you with me? You need to understand this step.*

_____12. Other _____

When planning your presentations, decide when you will pause to check for understanding. In your process speech, in which places could you break to check for understanding without greatly interrupting the flow of your speech?

*Examples 1–9 are taken from MICASE.

Asking for Questions

At strategic points in your speech, it's also important to ask the audience if they have any questions. Questions can serve to address uncertainties as well as provide additional information on your topic. Your answers can both enrich your speech and enhance your relationship with the audience. There are many ways speakers in academic settings elicit questions from the audience.

Task 13: Eliciting Questions

Read Examples 1–10.* Then answer the questions.

- In which examples does the speaker say that she welcomes questions from the audience?
- In which examples does the speaker address a particular member of the audience? Why?
- Which example cannot be used at the beginning or end of a speech?
- In which example does the speaker indicate that there is not much time for questions?
- What's the purpose of Example 10?

1. You can ask questions at any time.
2. Any questions or comments so far?**
3. Mary, did you have a question?
4. If you guys have any questions, feel free to ask.**
5. Okay, any other questions, (Ken)?**
6. Any questions before we move on?**
7. If you have any questions, just raise your hand, it's okay.
8. (I) would be happy to entertain a few brief questions.
9. So, any questions on that?**
10. Any more final questions?**

---

*Examples are from MICASE. Words in parentheses have been added.
**_Any questions?_ is commonly used to elicit questions from the audience. Notice that the auxiliary, subject, and verb _(Does anyone have)_ are often omitted.

Advantages to Using Computer Projection

1. Most presentations today are done using computer projection and PowerPoint slides because of the numerous options available for designing your visuals. Computer projection makes nonlinear presentations possible. You can easily skip both forward and backward to the images you want. You can also quickly add information to a slide as you speak. In addition, computer projectors can be used to produce audio, video, and animation. These features allow you to rethink how to present information.

    Keep in mind, however, that an eye-catching presentation using computer projection may still be criticized if it lacks such qualities as substance, a clear organizational strategy, a smooth flow, and audience considerations.

2. Color presentations can be easily made using computer projection; however, computer projection doesn't guarantee accurate color.

3. Presentations can be put on your flash drive or sent via the Internet.

4. If you have control of the lighting in both the front and back of the room, computer projectors may produce a clearer image.

5. If you have access to a computer projector with a remote control device, you have more flexibility regarding where you can stand.

6. Handouts that include your PowerPoint slides can be used by the audience for taking notes on your topic. They can also provide an option to your PowerPoint slides in case of an equipment failure. When using handouts, it's important to use good strategies for maintaining contact with the audience. Otherwise, audience members may stop paying attention to you and start reading through your handout.

Pronunciation

Intonation

In Unit 1, pausing was defined as slowing down or coming to a complete stop at a particular point. Unit 2 discussed stress. Words that convey important information are stressed or said more forcefully in English. Speakers who use proper pausing and stress are able to convey their message more effectively.

Intonation also plays a key role in communicating information to the audience. Intonation is the rise and fall of the pitch of our voices as we speak. In English, speakers most frequently use mid-level pitch. When our intonation rises from mid level, we are telling the listener that we have reached a word that we want to highlight. This rising intonation is accompanied by greater stress and pausing.

In this example, the speaker stresses the adjective, nouns, and verb in the utterance. In addition, the speaker highlights one word, *condenser,* by using a pattern of rising, then falling intonation within that word. The intonation rises from mid level to high level on the stressed (second) syllable of *condenser,* and then falls to low level on the last, unstressed syllable before coming to a stop.

The **coo**led **va**por **tra**vels to a *con**den**ser.* ///*

This rising and falling intonation on the last word in the utterance is common in English. One reason is that in English new important information is usually found toward the end, rather than at the beginning, of the sentence.

If the utterance is longer and has more than one pause, rising and falling intonation may also occur on a highlighted word before each pause.

Then after this step, // the cooled vapor travels to a condenser. ///

Notice that in this example, rising intonation does not occur on the last word before the pause (*step*) but on *this*. This is probably because the speaker wants to distinguish this step from other steps in the process. Since the speaker only slows during the first pause, rather than coming to a complete stop, the intonation doesn't fall to low level but returns to mid level, which saves the extra step of having to return to mid level from low level.

---

*// = slow down, /// = stop

As discussed in Unit 1, one type of pausing is coming to a full stop. However, remember that speaking is not like writing. In writing, there is a period (sometimes called a full stop) at the end of each sentence, but in speaking it isn't necessary to come to a full or complete stop. Instead, speakers can slow down as in the second example.

Then the vapor travels to a condenser. /// Inside it's condensed again. ///

Then the vapor travels to a condenser. // Inside, it's condensed again. ///

Notice that in the first example, the speaker pauses fully twice. When the speaker pauses fully, his intonation falls to low level.

In the second example, the speaker only slows down at *condenser*, which is why the intonation falls only to mid level and not to low level. The first utterance seems to flow into the second utterance. This is one way presenters speak faster in English. However, if listeners have trouble understanding, they may be able to hear and absorb the information better if the speaker pauses fully.

Task 14: Intonation Practice

Fill in the blanks and then practice saying this paragraph about yourself. Then say it out loud using rising intonation and then returning to mid level or low level.

My name is _____ and I'm from _____.

This year I'm studying _____ at _____.

I hope to get a job _____

_____. Before I came here, I _____

_____. In my free time,

I like to_____. I also like_____

_____.

Task 15: Self-Evaluation

With a partner, practice saying the paragraph on water treatment on page 63 or the introduction of your speech from Unit 2 or 3. Then evaluate yourself and each other. Do you think you have one or more of these problems? What challenges does this pose for listeners?

_____1. I don't stress key words enough. I seem to treat those words the same as other, less important words. It's like I have a different rhythm from native English speakers.

_____2. I use rising intonation too much. Usually, when I stress a word, my intonation rises. I'm constantly using rising intonation.

_____3. I speak too fast. I don't pause at natural breaks, such as at the end of a prepositional phrase, clause, or utterance. If I paused and also stressed key words more, I think I would automatically slow down.

_____4. When I speak, I pause a lot. They aren't at natural breaks, so my speech sounds choppy. I say words individually but need to think about them as part of a group of words.

_____5. Other: _____

Task 16: Your Stress and Intonation Patterns

Read the paragraph on water treatment on page 63. This time record it. Mark the stress and intonation pattern you used. If you wish to alter your stress and intonation pattern, make adjustments and record it again.

Task 17: Process Presentation

Give a five- to six-minute speech that describes a process in your field. Choose a topic that interests a general academic audience that you can discuss within the time limit. If you choose a topic that is too technical or too simple, your audience will lose interest.

1. Include an attention-getting opening. Pose a rhetorical question to the listeners. Also ask yourself what background information the audience needs in order to understand the process.

2. Decide what time connectors you will use to make your speech easier for the audience to follow. Use the signpost *let's* as a linking word to connect steps in your process if appropriate.

3. As you plan the steps in your process, ask yourself whether a step is best described using the active voice, passive voice, or both. Eliminate unnecessary modals. If you are giving a series of instructions, consider using commands (imperatives), *you* followed by a verb, and appropriate modals.

4. Plan to stop your speech at strategic breaks, such as at the end of your introduction or after a step, to check for understanding or to answer questions.

5. Before giving your speech, practice it at least two to three times. Then record it at least once and evaluate yourself using the evaluation form on pages 91–92. Be sure to include a critique of your non-verbal behavior. Then practice your presentation several more times.

6. Unless you are giving a demonstration, use one or several visuals to enhance your presentation. They will help you (1) maintain the audience's attention, (2) ensure that the audience is following you, and (3) remember what you are going to say. Evaluate your visuals with a classmate using the checklist on page 90. If you answer yes to any of the questions, make appropriate changes.

7. Review the information on using computer projection and the blackboard.

VISUAL EVALUATION	YES	NO
1. Are any visuals missing a title?		
2. Is there too much written information on any of the visuals?		
3. Is any writing too small to see?		
4. Are any important parts unlabeled?		
5. Are any of the visuals unorganized, confusing, or cluttered?		
6. Can the visuals be altered to make them more eye-catching?		
7. Do any of the visuals contain information not covered in the speech?		

Process Speech Evaluation

Process Speech Evaluation Form

Name: _____

	(Make a check in the appropriate column)			
	Good	OK	Needs Work	Comments (include specific problems you noticed)
Topic information Interesting process? Appropriate for a general academic audience?				
Introduction Used a rhetorical question or another attention-getting device? Provided useful background information before describing the process? Explained the relevance or importance of the process? Carefully organized introductory information?				
Process Clearly organized steps?				
Transitions Used time connectors and other words and phrases like *let's* to signal moves from one part of the process to another?				
Definitions Provided definitions of key terms that may have been unfamiliar to the listeners?				
Grammar Used correct tense and voice to explain steps in the process or the imperative if necessary? Used modals with *you* when they served a clear purpose?				

| | (Make a check in the appropriate column) | | | |
	Good	OK	Needs Work	Comments (include specific problems you noticed)
Pace Not too fast or slow? Smooth rather than hesitant, choppy?				
Eye contact Maintained eye contact with all listeners?				
Gestures Hands were free and expressive?				
Volume Spoke loud enough for everyone to hear without straining?				
Interaction with audience Checked for understanding? Requested questions from the audience?				
Use of Equipment Used computer projection and/or the blackboard/whiteboard effectively?				

Pronunciation
(specific problems)

Other comments

Goals for my next presentation (list 2–3 areas that you want to improve for your next presentation)

Unit 4 ———————————————————————

Defining a Concept

In this unit, you will present an extended definition of a concept from your field of study. In a sense, you have already given two extended definition speeches. When you described an object, you elaborated on the basic definition of the object by describing its physical characteristics and discussing the functions of its different parts. When you described a process, you extended the definition of the process by describing each of the steps in the process. This unit will discuss additional ways to extend the basic definition of a concept.

Definitions are very common in academic discourse. We encounter them when we read textbooks and academic papers. We also hear them when we attend class lectures and department talks. In fact, it is difficult to imagine a lecture that does not contain a definition either as part of the speaker's text or in response to a question.

You may need to give an oral definition as part of

❐ a class discussion
❐ a meeting with your study or research group
❐ a formal or informal talk
❐ an oral examination or thesis defense

Defining is describing the unique, distinguishing properties of a concept in a particular context. In an academic environment, definitions can be important when words have one meaning in "everyday" English but another meaning in a specialized field of study. For example, *appreciation* can refer to grateful feelings, but in business it refers to the increase in the value of land or other possessions. In addition, words may have different meanings depending on one's field of study. In dentistry, for instance, *enamel* is the hard outer covering of our teeth, while in materials science, *enamel* is an opaque coating that is baked on metal or ceramic.

Some terms can often be defined in one sentence or even one word. However, when you define an important concept in your field, your goal may be to extend its basic definition by providing more specific information or details so that the listener has a richer understanding of its meaning.

Task 1: Defining a Battery

How would you define a battery? Working in pairs or small groups, read the speech aloud. Think about how the speaker has chosen to develop the definition. Then answer the questions on page 96.

Definition of a Battery

① Okay, imagine yourself in this situation: You're going across campus to a class. Uh, you're walking with a student of the opposite sex from your department who's going to the same class. All of a sudden, this person's spouse, who who turns out to be really jealous, comes up and like punches you in the nose.

② It turns out that your nose is broken, and um by the time you finish paying all your medical expenses, your bill adds up to over one thousand dollars. You want the spouse to pay for the damages you suffered. In this situation, damages is compensation for your financial loss. Okay? [*The speaker writes* damages *on the blackboard.*]

③ So you go to the student legal services office, and uh uh the lawyer there tells you that you might be able to sue the spouse for damages under a legal theory or principle called a battery. [*The speaker reveals the title of the presentation.*]

④ So, what's a battery? A battery is intentional touching of another person. [*The speaker reveals this information on a slide.*] A battery is intentional touching of another person. [*The speaker points to the words on the screen.*] Let me explain what I mean by intentional touching.

⑤ There are a lot of social situations where we intentionally touch each other, you know for example when we shake hands or tap someone on the shoulder. But, uh, a battery is intentional touching that's harmful or offensive, like hitting or punching someone. [*The speaker continues to reveal information on the slide(s).*]

⑥ In addition, to recover damages or, um, get um get compensation, the touching must cause injury. Injury is defined in two ways: physical injury and injury to someone's dignity. An example of physical injury is a head concussion. An example of an injury to someone's dignity would be, um, an insult to a person's race or nationality.

⑦ So, a battery is intentional touching. It's harmful or offensive touching, and uh it causes physical injury or injury to someone's dignity. Everybody understand so far? [*Audience answers yes.*]

⑧ Let's focus for a minute on the term *touching*. In law, a battery also extends to, uh, intentional offensive touching that involves indirect contact. By *indirect,* I mean contact with something that is touching you, like the books you're carrying or the clothes you're wearing. I mean, for example, suppose someone comes up and grabs the h- um, um, hood of your jacket and drags you to the ground, but doesn't actually touch you. That's indirect contact. Okay?

⑨ The definition of battery also extends to, uh, to what is called *causing to touch*. For instance, you come into class and begin to sit down in your desk but someone pulls the desk out from under you and and you fall on the floor. Even though the person didn't touch you, he or she caused you to touch the floor.

⑩ So, the definition of touching can include um indirect contact or causing a person to to touch something.

⑪ Okay. Now let's go back to our hypothetical broken-nose situation. Let me ask you some questions:

- Did the spouse intend to touch you? [*Audience answers yes.*]

- And was the touching ha-harm-harmful or offensive? [*Audience answers yes, harmful.*]

- By the way, um what kind of touching was it? I mean was it direct or indirect? [*Audience answers direct.*]

- Did you suffer injury? [*Audience answers yes, physical injury, a broken nose.*]

  [*Speaker reveals slide.*]

⑫ Since the answer to these four questions is yes, then the spouse may have committed a battery and you may be able to receive damages to cover your medical costs.

⑬ So, does everyone have a general understanding of what a battery is? Yes? Any final questions?

Discussion Questions

1. How does the speaker begin the speech?

2. In what section does the speaker begin the actual definition? How does she begin the section?

3. In Section 4, why does the speaker repeat the definition?

4. How does the speaker extend the definition of *battery*?

5. What kind of audience is the speaker addressing—a group of law students or a more general academic audience?

6. What are some strategies that the speaker uses to maintain a relationship with the audience throughout the speech?

7. The speaker uses *okay* several times in the presentation. Look at Sections 1, 2, and 11. How is *okay* used?

8. What's the purpose of *so* in Sections 3, 7, and 13? Could the speaker have used *okay* instead of *so* in Sections 7 and 13?

9. The speaker uses two slides. On the first slide, she first reveals the title and then reveals Numbers 1–5 as she discusses them. The speaker puts the test on the second slide. What's your opinion of this strategy?

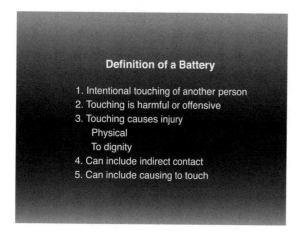

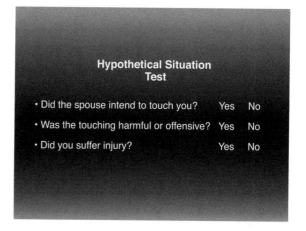

In the speech, the speaker maintains a relationship with the audience by using several strategies.

- ❐ She begins with a hypothetical story that includes the audience.
- ❐ She uses a rhetorical question to introduce the concept she is defining.
- ❐ She repeats the basic definition of *battery* in case members of the audience didn't understand it the first time.
- ❐ As she goes through each element or essential part of a battery, she uses examples to clarify what she means.
- ❐ She defines other unknown terms.
- ❐ She stops several times along the way to check if the audience is following. She also asks the audience if they have questions.
- ❐ She summarizes what she has said so far during her speech.
- ❐ She tests the audience's understanding of *battery* by asking them questions. She asks the audience to decide if a battery has taken place.

The speaker is likely speaking to an audience with little academic legal knowledge. If she were speaking to listeners with a legal background, she might choose a different way to present the topic. In addition, her style is somewhat instructional. She treats her speech like a class lesson. This strategy helps her develop more interaction with the audience members.

Notice that in this speech, the speaker uses *okay* in three different ways. One is to announce to the audience that the speech is going to begin (Section 1). Another is to check with the audience to make sure they are following (Section 2). The third is to let the audience know that the speaker is going to go on to a new section of the speech (Section 11). The speaker uses *so* throughout the speech. Three common ways she uses *so* are to show result (Section 3), to summarize (Section 7), and to conclude (Section 13).

Task 2: Fillers

You may have noticed that when the speaker paused during her speech, she sometimes repeated words or inserted sounds, words, or parts of words that didn't add to the content of her speech. These are called *fillers*. Look at the examples and circle the fillers that the speaker inserted.

1. Uh, you're walking with a student of the opposite sex from your department who's going to the same class.

2. All of a sudden, this person's spouse, who, who turns out to be really jealous, comes up and like punches you in the nose.

3. There are a lot of social situations where we intentionally touch each other, you know for example when we shake hands or tap someone on the shoulder.

4. By *indirect* I mean contact with something that was touching you, like the books you're carrying or the clothes you're wearing. I mean, for example, suppose someone comes up and grabs the h- um, um, hood of your jacket and drags you to the ground, but doesn't actually touch you. That's indirect contact.

5. For instance, you come into class and begin to sit down in your desk but someone pulls the desk out from under you and and you fall on the floor.

6. And was the touching ha-harm-harmful or offensive?

Task 3: Comparing Speakers´ Use of Fillers

Read the first excerpt* about juggling work and family given by a professor to a group of students interested in teaching at the college level. Then read the second excerpt* about public safety by a university instructor in a classroom setting. Underline or circle the fillers that they use. What similarities and differences do you notice? Discuss the number of fillers the speakers use.

EXCERPT 1

I do have three young children so, a-as a rule, I I try to get home at a decent hour. So we have meals, and, uh, and then play with my kids. I make an honest attempt to get 'em to bed by nine o'clock. Uh, so, uh, usually till about nine nine-thirty, it's primarily consumed by, you know, spending time with family, eating and, you know, and, and, and hanging around with the kids.

EXCERPT 2

There is not much evidence that there has been any sort of public safety benefit from deterrence or from incapacitation. And, you know, though the person locked up, uh, can't commit a crime, we all know that, uh, uh, that somebody will take his or her place out in the world and, and, and cause the same level of mayhem that that, that, the person locked up would've caused.

*Excerpts from MICASE, with minor changes.

Fillers like *um* and *uh* and even repetitions like *uh uh, and and,* and *ha-harm-harmful* are a normal part of spoken presentations. One reason speakers use fillers is to give themselves a space for thinking what they're going to say next. However, when you evaluate your speech, if you feel that you have too many fillers and pauses, you may need to practice more to sound more fluent. Fillers such as *like, you know,* and *I mean* are rather informal. Their overuse may make a speaker seem unprepared. They are also potentially confusing to the listener because they have other meanings. Even though they are used extensively in casual conversation, speakers should attempt to limit their use in more formal presentations. (In Number 4 on page 98, compare the two uses of *I mean.*)

Discussion Question

1. What fillers from your own language do you find yourself using when you speak English? Could any of them potentially distract listeners or interfere with the audience's comprehension?

Developing or Extending a Definition

In the Definition of a Battery speech, the speaker gives both a brief definition of *battery* and a more complete definition. The speaker continues to refine the definition even further, using examples to clarify each refinement. This is only one approach. There are many other ways to develop or extend a definition.

The list on page 101 summarizes common ways a speaker can extend a definition. Definition speeches may contain one or more of these. Which types have you used in the speeches you've already given?

Organizing Extended Definitions

After choosing a topic and deciding what information you want to include in your extended definition, you will need to organize the information. Topics may lend themselves to a specific organization pattern or patterns. For example, in the battery presentation, the speaker defines *injury* by categorizing it into two different types. If you chose biofuel as your topic, you could define it by comparing and contrasting it with fossil fuels. Then you may want to list the various kinds of biofuels and then compare and contrast them.

Listing

❑ enumerate characteristics, features
❑ provide examples
❑ list applications

Spatial Order

❑ relate the location of objects and their parts in space

Classification

❑ introduce two or more different categories or types

Chronological Order

❑ describe how something is made, created, or has evolved
❑ discuss how something works, is carried out, or develops
❑ outline the history or evolution of the concept, including its future potential
❑ exemplify by telling a story or anecdote
❑ discuss habitual behavior

Comparison and Contrast

❑ compare with another phenomenon, development, concept, activity, person, or object
❑ discuss competing definitions

The organizational pattern(s) you choose will suggest connecters that can be used to create a smooth coherent flow of speech.

Task 4: Choosing an Organizational Pattern

Working in groups or with a partner, choose several words from the list
and discuss how you would extend your definition of each of them. Which
organizational patterns would you use? Add a word from your field of studies in
the last row and discuss how you would extend it.

Word/Phrase	Possible Ways to Extend the Definition
friction	
microenterprise	
tornado	
folk art	
pagoda	
cement composite	
solar panel	
organic farming	
artificial muscle	
opera	
hummingbird	

Task 5: Organizational Patterns in Extended Definitions

Read the definitions. Decide what main organizational pattern each speaker uses. Discuss other interesting features of these definitions.

1. The **definition** of work changed from labor in the household performed by everybody to waged labor—labor for which wages were paid outside the home—so that gradually the notion of women's work (at home) gets erased. It's not paid labor in the home, and so it no longer is considered work.

2. Stress is just basically **defined** as a reaction of the mind and body against change. The change doesn't have to be an unpleasant one. It could be a good change, a bad change. It's just something that your body's not ready to face that creates stress. And it produces bodily or mental tension. It's caused by pressure to meet demands or, just things that your body isn't ready to uh face. There're mainly three types of stress. The first is mechanical stress and that's caused by physical factors like lifting heavy objects, exercising too much or not exercising enough. Uh mental stress is caused by emotional aspects or social aspects and that's uh like not getting enough sleep or marriage problems, relationship problems, work problems, things like that. And finally there's chemical stress which is a much broader category but it's mostly a chemical input uh in your body and environmental factors, So it's caused by pollution or um fumes from your furniture or carpets, things you may not think that could cause stress but they do.

3. Epidemiology is seen as a completely objective science that focuses on associations that are very clearly specified. It uses variables that are very precisely defined and the way it looks at those associations is through things like measurement and counting, and statistical analysis. So one **definition** of epidemiology might be the scientific assessment of clearly specified associations, among precisely defined variables, through measurement and counting and statistical analysis. Anthropology, by contrast, is uh is thought of as a subjective discipline. It's thought of as devoted to understanding the inner worlds of other people. And it does so by means of very close, very empathetic, encounters.

4. One anthropologist, um, Brenda Williams, has talked about the difference between making a living and making life. And what does she mean by that? She talks about how different groups talk about each other in these terms. So for instance, Indian shopkeepers, who are the people who have started most of the shops in this community. They are talked about as being very very good at making a living, but not terribly good at making life. People say they work all the time. And so they don't have time to actually live life. So, she draws that distinction. Making a living is **defined as** a person's industry, skill or ambition, all of which result in material awards, whereas making life is your interest in the socioeconomic well-being of others as well as your own.*

---

*Excerpts from MICASE, with minor modifications.

Opening a Definition Speech

In the Definition of a Battery speech, the speaker began by describing a hypothetical situation rather than beginning with *Today, I'm going to define* battery. In fact, she didn't introduce *battery* until Section 4. One purpose of the hypothetical situation is to get the audience interested in the topic. Another is to place the word in a context. There are many effective ways to open a definition speech. However, the concept you define may be more suited to one type of opening than another. In addition, the audience and purpose of the speech may influence the type of opening you choose.

Task 6: Examining Speech Introductions

Read the four introductions to definition speeches and discuss with a partner or group how the speakers began their presentations. Then discuss how the speakers might extend their definitions.

1. If you've gone camping before, you've probably had to take along a lot of equipment and supplies. One common camping supply that campers are familiar with is dehydrated food. By dehydrated food, I mean food that has had most of its moisture taken out. As a result, it weighs less, which makes it ideal for camping trips. So, dehydration is the process of removing moisture from food. Dehydration also preserves food because it retards enzyme action, which makes it safer to eat. Food has been preserved for centuries by means of dehydration. Today, five modern methods are used to dehydrate food.

2. How many of you have to wear glasses or contact lenses? Five of you. Actually, I can think of one time that all of you have to wear glasses— that's when you watch a movie in 3-D. If you don't wear glasses, the picture looks blurry. Three-D or three-dimensional films are films shot using two different cameras placed next to each other.

3. What does *wife* mean? The *American Heritage Dictionary* defines *wife* as "a woman married to a man." However, in law, *wife* can be considered a legal term since a woman who gets married enters into a legal relationship that can alter her rights. In American law, the definition of *wife* has changed over time mainly because a wife's legal rights have changed.

4.
   each day an Autumn . . .

   fire and sweetness in your hearts

   apples on the stove

   The type of poem I just read is called haiku. Haiku is a three-line poem containing a total of seventeen syllables, five in the first line, seven in the second, and five in the third. (Haiku by Niki Ford.)

5. Have any of you ever seen a volcano? What about on TV? You've probably seen the results of a volcanic eruption and are aware that it can have serious consequences. A volcano can disrupt air travel; destroy houses, roads, and farmland; cause serious health problems; and kill humans and animals. But there's something potentially far more devastating than a volcano—a supervolcano. A supervolcano is a volcano that's capable of producing an eruption many times greater than any volcanic eruption that's occurred in our lifetime.

Strategies for Opening Your Speech

Read the list of strategies for opening a definition speech. A speaker may decide to use more than one strategy. These strategies may also be helpful when designing openings to other types of speeches as a means of getting the audience's attention and establishing the context. Add some of your own.

1. a rhetorical question
2. a question to the audience that is meant to elicit a response
3. a hypothetical situation or short anecdote
4. an example
5. an opening statement that places the concept in a context
6. historical background
7. a picture
8. music or other sounds
9. a quote, a poem, or a saying
10. _____
11. _____

Task 7: Designing a Speech Opening

Choose a term from your field. Write an attention-getting opening for your speech that is compatible with the term you have chosen. Share it with a partner or small group. Then discuss ways in which you might extend your definition.

Term:

Speech opening:

Ways to expand the definition and organizational pattern (patterns):

Formal Definitions

In academic writing, a writer frequently introduces a term to be defined with a one-sentence three-part definition. In academic speaking, the presenter may use a three-part definition or may prefer a more informal method. The three parts of a formal definition are

- ❏ the term
- ❏ the class in which the term belongs
- ❏ the characteristics that distinguish it from other terms in the class

Task 8: Three-Part Definitions

Read the definitions and underline the three parts of each definition.

(term)   (class)   (distinguishing characteristics)

1. A <u>membrane</u> is a <u>thin wall</u> that <u>allows certain types of substances</u> to pass through.

2. A battery is harmful or offensive touching that causes physical injury or injury to someone's dignity.

3. An herbicide is a chemical substance that is used to kill unwanted plants.

4. An equilateral triangle is a triangle/one that has sides of equal length.

5. Loam is a type of soil that primarily consists (soil primarily consisting) of sand, clay, silt, and other organic matter.

6. A cataract is an eye abnormality in which the lens becomes opaque, causing blindness.

7. A seismoscope is a device that measures the time an earthquake occurs.

Notice that definitions follow certain formats or use similar grammatical structures.

- ❏ The distinguishing characteristics are contained in the relative clause that begins with *that* or *which* (Sentences 1–5) or a preposition plus *which* (Sentence 6).

- ❏ It may also be possible to use a part of the term as the class or *one* (such as triangle/*one* in Sentence 4), especially if the word is well known.

- ❏ Sometimes it is possible to use a reduced relative clause (*soil consisting* in Sentence 5). How could you reduce the definition of *herbicide* in Sentence 3 and the definition of *equilateral triangle* in Sentence 4?

Task 9: Additional Ways to Define a Term

Read these examples of other ways to introduce the term *seismograph* in spoken academic English. How do they differ from the three-part formal definition on page 108. How are they similar? Are any less formal? Explain. Are they all appropriate for an academic presentation?

1. What's the definition of seismograph? It's a device you use to detect and record earthquakes.

2. By seismograph, I mean a device that detects an earthquake.

3. The U.S. Geological Survey (2012) defines seismograph as a device that detects and records earthquakes.

4. A seismograph is gonna keep a record when an earthquake occurs.

Task 10: Examining Definitions in Task 6

Review the five openings of definition speeches in Task 6 (pages 105–6). Find the concept(s) that each speaker introduced and defined. Which speakers used a three-part definition? What other forms did speakers choose?

Defining Additional Terms

In the Definition of a Battery speech, you noticed that in order to fully define *battery*, the speaker used words that are unfamiliar to the audience. In order to be certain the listeners are following, the speaker also defines these additional, unfamiliar terms. She tries to make the definitions as short as possible so as not to interrupt the flow of the speech. These short definitions are sometimes referred to as *substitutions*. There are four main types of substitutions.

Substitution	Meaning	Example
Synonym	One or several words that have the same or a similar meaning	*A camera has an aperture or hole where the light passes through.*
Paraphrase	Words that clarify or explain the meaning of a term by rephrasing it	*Rheumatoid arthritis is an auto-immune disease—a disease in which the body's defense mechanism turns against itself.* *The materials are translucent—in other words, light can pass through them.*
Example	Representatives of the term	*Flooring can be made of hardwood—oak, cherry, maple, and so on.*
Acronym	Initials or letters that stand for a longer term	*Liquid crystal displays, or LCDs,* . . .*

*If the acronym is commonly used, such as RADAR, the speaker may begin with the initials and then explain what they stand for.

Task 11: Substitutions

Read the terms from the Definition of a Battery speech. Identify the type of substitution the speaker uses to define each italicized term.

1. _____ The lawyer tells you that you might be able to sue under a legal *theory* or principle called a battery.

2. _____ For instance, an *injury to someone's dignity* would be an insult to a person's race or nationality.

3. _____ In this situation, *damages* is compensation for financial loss.

4. _____ A battery also extends to intentional offensive touching that involves *indirect contact,* in other words, contact with something that was touching you, like the books you were carrying or the clothes you were wearing.

Task 12: Adhesion and Cohesion

Read the speech on adhesion and cohesion. Then, working in small groups, answer the questions on page 114. The speaker is using the audience for a first run of her speech, which she'll give in an education class.

Hi, Everybody.

As you know, I'm planning to be a science education teacher in public school. I've prepared a lesson on cohesion and adhesion *aimed at elementary school students in around 6th grade. I'd like your feedback before I present it to my education class this week. Mainly, what do you think about it? Should I add or change anything for sixth graders? Are there any inaccuracies? How about my style? Okay, here goes.*

① Imagine that you've put a drop of honey between your thumb and your forefinger and you're rubbing it around. How does it feel? Yes, sticky. How do you know when something is sticky? Right, it's not as easy to remove as some other things like water. Now, what if I put a piece of paper between my thumb and forefinger and then open my finger and thumb. What happens? The paper falls. Why does the paper fall and the honey stay on my finger and thumb?

② It's because the honey has adhesive qualities that cause it to cling to or adhere to my finger and thumb. But the paper has what we call strong cohesive qualities, which means that it holds itself together really well. So, cohesion has to do with how well a substance can "stick to itself"—in other words, how strong the molecules of a substance are bonded together. Adhesion has to do with how well something can stick to something else. In other words, how strong the molecular attraction between the two different substances is.

③ Let's go back to the honey for a minute. When you open your thumb and finger, where is the honey? Yes, it's on both the finger and the thumb. In this case, its adhesive properties cause honey to continue to stick to your finger and thumb. Honey's cohesive ability is not very strong, which is why the honey separates and ends up on both your finger and thumb.

④ Which of these objects have strong cohesive properties? And which have strong adhesive properties? Water, gum, a rock.

⑤ Let's look at water. Can a water drop on a piece of metal maintain its shape, at least for a while? Yes. But if you put your hand on it, it doesn't. That's because water is somewhat adhesive. A rock has far more cohesion. It is much less likely to adhere to something. What about a piece of gum? If you chew it and then put it between your finger and thumb, it would likely stick to one side or both if it is soft enough. But if gum sits around and gets really hard, it might become more cohesive. That means it's not as sticky as it used to be and there's a chance it might not stick to either your thumb or finger. In general, solids are more cohesive than liquids and liquids are more adhesive.

⑥ A number of methods are used commercially to test how adhesive a product is. But you can do some simple tests at home. For example, take two pieces of wood and glue them together. After the glue dries, see if you can separate the two pieces of wood. Then take two identical pieces of wood and glue them together with another type of glue. Which glue adheres better to the wood? In other words, which has the higher adhesive strength? Here you've used force as your test method.

⑦ Another test you can do it to put some paint and a drop of candle wax on a piece of glass. Let them dry and then take a scraper and try to scrape them off. You can use your fingernail if you want. Which one is the hardest to remove? In other words, which one has the higher adhesive strength? Here you're using scraping as your test method.

So, does everyone have a good idea of what cohesion and adhesion are? Can you give me some more examples? What about a way you test the strength of an adhesive?

Discussion Questions

1. Do you find it hard to explain concepts and ideas from your area of studies to people who are not in that field? What strategies do you use to simplify information so that a generalist can understand it?

2. What approach does the speaker use to develop her *cohesion* and *adhesion* presentation for the audience she'll be addressing? Would you suggest another approach? What about if she were teaching high school students?

3. What specific strategies does the speaker use to keep in touch with the audience?

4. How would you change this explanation if you were speaking before an audience of university students? How might graduate students be more likely to discuss this topic?

5. How enjoyable was this speech for you? Did it make a difference if you already know all the information in the speech?

6. What feedback would you give the speaker about her presentation? Before giving a presentation, do you do a "dry run" with someone who can critique you?

The presenter gives a definition speech in which she compares two terms, *adhesion* and *cohesion*. She's not speaking to her intended audience. Her intended audience is her education class and ultimately her elementary school students. She gives some nice examples of the difference between cohesion and adhesion and how an ordinary person might test the strength of an adhesive. She doesn't, however, get into a more complex discussion of either of these two topics since it might lead to a more in-depth scientific explanation, unfamiliar vocabulary, and mathematics. When deciding on how complex to make a presentation, audience can be a key factor.

Task 13: Using Narratives in Extended Definitions

Read the narratives from a botany lecture and a psychology lecture. Discuss the speaker's purpose in using these narratives. Point out similarities between the two lectures.

1. Practical Botany Lecture.* In this lecture, the professor tells a story about a pizza delivery driver who falls over a rosebush.

   A pizza delivery kid backed his car into the driveway of my neighbor. You know how sometimes they're a little sloppy getting parked. And he got out of his car, and he tripped over something, and he fell, pizzas and all, right on a rosebush, and really did a lot of damage to those pizzas and to himself and to that rosebush. And he was so flummoxed *(confused)* by all of this that he got into his vehicle and backed out of the yard as fast as he could go, driving right over the rosebush. And you know what? The next spring that rosebush came back to life and grew, thrived, and had roses. And you could say that that rosebush was pretty hardy, to be able to endure all of this stuff. And if you said that, you'd probably be right in some vernacular *(common, nontechnical)* sense. But you wouldn't be right as a gardener, unless what the rosebush really had done was survive the cold winter because to gardeners *hardy* means the ability to tolerate cold. Now plants are rated on their ability to tolerate cold.

*From MICASE, with modifications.

2.　Introduction to Psychology Lecture.* In this lecture, a professor mentions his son, Michael, and how they watched a program on the Discovery Channel about a fish that divers found 300 feet below the ocean's surface.

> Often people think about natural selection as being this all-knowing, guided, planful thing out there, as though natural selection has a grand plan for each of us and it's gonna determine what things are good and what things are bad. Um, in fact last night I was watching *(television)* with Michael. We were flipping through the Discovery Channel, and they had a program on about these guys who were diving down to three hundred feet underneath the water trying to find a species of fish. And they found this one incredibly ugly fish. It looked like a bowling ball, only it was a really ugly bowling ball, and it had lost its ability to swim. What it did was walked across the bottom, on its little fins, so its fins were useless now. It was just this big beach-bally kind of thing. Useless for swimming but good for walking, right? And the narrator on this *[program]* made this statement, which just almost sent me over the edge. The narrator said, evolution has taken care of two problems at once. While taking away the ability to swim it has given the fish the ability to walk on the bottom, as though evolution knew what the hell it was doing, right? Evolution doesn't know what it's doing. That's not what evolution is about. Evolution is a probabilistic occurrence. Basically what evolution boils down to is that it says that things that work are gonna be more common, and things that don't work in a particular environment are gonna be less common. If the environment changes, evolution doesn't know that, right? So if the environment changes, something that at one point worked really well doesn't work anymore. If it doesn't work anymore, it's gonna be selected against. So there's always this temptation to think that evolution is moving us in the direction towards always higher performance. That's not what evolution is doing at all. Evolution is a pressure to match your characteristics with your environment, and really not *your* characteristics, your *offspring*'s characteristics. Evolution is a theory about how environments shape organisms over time. Okay?

*From MICASE, with modifications.

Concluding Your Speech

Many speakers who carefully plan and practice their speeches still find themselves at a loss at the end of their presentation because they are unsure how to conclude their speeches. They may end their speeches abruptly (e.g., *that's all*) or may drag out their speech by making several attempts to conclude.

Task 14: Evaluating Conclusions

Read the ten speech endings. Working in pairs or small groups, discuss the strategies that the speakers used to conclude their speeches. Place a check mark (✔) next to the ones you think are the most effective. Place an X in front of those you think are the least effective. Be prepared to explain your choices.

_____ 1. So, that's all I have to say about polymers.

_____ 2. That's the end of my speech on polymers. Thanks for listening. I know it was hard to understand.

_____ 3. Today I've defined the term polymer. I've discussed the characteristics of polymers and have explained the different types of polymers. I've also given you examples of polymers. Do you have any questions?

_____ 4. Now I think you're able to understand why the characteristics of polymers lend themselves to creating many of the products that we use in our homes today. Any final questions?

_____ 5. In summary, the harp is a unique instrument. You can see how different it is. None of the other musical instruments are like the harp. Thank you.

_____ 6. In conclusion, today I've described the major parts of the harp and their functions. Any questions?

_____ 7. So that's a simple description of the major parts of the harp and their functions. What you haven't been able to hear today is the beautiful sound the harp makes. Hopefully, you'll have the chance to hear the harp being played at one of the Music School's concerts this semester. Any questions?

_____ 8. So today I've discussed the major parts of a deciduous tree and their functions. Next time I'll discuss the process by which deciduous trees lose their leaves each year. Any final questions?

_____ 9. So that's my brief introduction to how the Rankine Cycle works.

_____ 10. So, if you have children, the next time you take them to a 3-D movie, you'll be able to tell them how it was made.

Tips for Concluding Your Presentation

Before you design a conclusion for your speech:

> Choose a strategy (strategies) that is compatible with the purpose and goals of your speech.

  ▶ Briefly summarize what you said in your speech.

  ▶ Tie your conclusion to a question you asked or a statement you made at the beginning of your speech.

  ▶ Stress the importance of your topic in the listeners' daily lives.

  ▶ Leave the audience with a question to think about.

  ▶ End with a recommendation.

  ▶ Briefly mention something that you weren't able to include in your presentation and that you hope to discuss in a future presentation.

  ▶ Re-emphasize the far-ranging impact or the elegance of your solution.

  ▶ End with a humorous statement related to your topic.

> Weigh if it is necessary to repeat information from your speech or if this repetition will detract from your presentation.

> Consider the length of your conclusion (does it need to be more than two or three sentences?).

Using Visuals with Outlines

Look at the slides that the speaker made for the Definition of a Battery presentation on page 96. Many presentations begin with an outline. A speech outline can be beneficial to both the audience and the speaker for these reasons:

❑ It helps the audience follow the speaker's chosen organizational pattern.

❑ It helps the speaker remember what she or he is going to say.

❑ Providing key words and major points helps listeners understand better.

Task 15: Designing a Visual

Read the information presented on a slide for a speech defining the word *polymer*. Then, working in small groups, answer the questions on page 120.

Introduction to Polymers

What is a polymer?

Characteristics of polymers

Molecular structures of polymers
- Linear
- Branched
- Network

Classifications of polymers
- Thermoplastics
- Rubbers
- Thermosets

Examples of polymers

Conclusion

Discussion Questions

1. How will the speaker extend the definition of *polymer*?

2. If you were giving a presentation, how could you present the information on a PowerPoint slide?

3. How could the information be improved by adding pictures? Explain.

Maintaining Contact with the Audience

Let me (lemme)

Let me, which is pronounced *lemme* in fast speech, is commonly used by the speaker to tell the listeners what he or she is going to do. Notice that in the Definition of a Battery speech, the speaker uses *Let me* two times.

> *Let me explain what I mean by intentional touching.*
>
> *Let me ask you some questions.*

Task 16: Using *Let me*

What is the speaker going to after each of the statements?

1. Let me write, I'm going to write [the words on the board].

   _____

2. Let me add just one more thing.

   _____

3. Let me backtrack here.

   _____

4. Lemme give you a little background.

   _____

5. Let me digress.

   _____

6. Let me just rephrase this.

   _____

7. Lemme just give you a few more statistics.

   _____

8. Let me go on.

   _____

9. Let me close . . . .

   _____

10. Let me answer your question in a minute.*

   _____

Let's cannot be used in place of *Let me* if speakers see themselves as acting on their own. Compare *Let me think of another example* to *Let's think of another example.* In the second example, the speaker is inviting the audience to participate in the process.

---

*Examples 1–9 are from MICASE. Words in brackets have been added.

Interrupting the Speaker

By encouraging audience members to ask questions or ask for clarification, speakers are giving them a role in the presentation. Unless the speaker has asked the audience to hold questions until the end of the presentation, listeners can get the speaker's attention by raising their hand. However, if the audience is small and the situation informal, listeners may be able to politely interrupt the speaker. In both cases, verbal expressions that accompany the interruption* include

> *I'm sorry. A what topic?*
>
> *Could you repeat that, please?*
>
> *I didn't get/catch that.*
>
> *I wonder if you could explain . . .*
>
> *Excuse me. I'm not following this.*
>
> *I'm just a bit confused.*

—Discussion Questions—

1. Which examples seem to be asking for a brief clarification from the speaker?

2. What expressions do the speakers use to soften the interruption or make a polite request?

3. What does *I didn't get/catch that* mean?

4. Can you use *I wonder* and *I was wondering* interchangeably?

5. Notice that only one audience member uses *please* when she interrupts. What other ways can you make a polite request in English?

*Items are adapted from MICASE.

The strategies that speakers use to soften interruptions include *I'm sorry, Excuse me, I wonder, Could you. . . .* In English, *please* can have the potential for being less polite, so speakers often avoid using it when interrupting. Notice that the speaker uses *please* in only one example but accompanies it with the softener *could you.*

Professors may use *please* to give instructions to their class, as in *Please get your homework to me next week* or *please pick up your lecture quizzes.**

Pronunciation

Intonation and Noun Phrases

Unit 3 discussed intonation and how speakers use rising intonation to highlight words in English. One challenge that faces nonnative speakers of English is choosing the correct intonation pattern when highlighting certain noun phrases.

Look at the pairs of noun phrases. What is the difference between the noun phrases in Column 1 and the corresponding noun phrases in Column 2?

Column 1	Column 2
1. telephone equipment	modern equipment
2. a childhood disease	a common disease
3. health care	adequate care
4. a system failure	a major failure
5. his career interests	his current interests
6. an engineering study	a new study

In the first noun phrase of each pair, the noun phrase is composed of two nouns, the first functioning as an adjective:

> *noun functioning as adjective + noun*

Consider gerunds, such as *engineering, teaching, swimming, housing,* as nouns.

In the second noun phrase of each pair, the noun phrase consists of an adjective and a noun:

> *adjective + noun*

---

*In this example, notice that the leader of a campus tour uses *please* to insist that everyone stop talking and pay attention to him: *I got a couple quick,* **please** *listen to me,* **please please please** *listen to me,* **please** *listen to me, thank you. I got a couple quick administrative things to go through real quick* (MICASE, 2000).

In English, both nouns in Column 1 are stressed, and in Column 2 both the adjective and noun are stressed because they all provide important information to the listener. However, the intonation pattern of these two types of noun phrase differs.

Read these general guidelines for intonation with noun phrases in English. When the noun phrase consists of a noun + noun combination, rising intonation generally occurs on the stressed syllable of the noun that is functioning as an adjective (*telephone, childhood, health*). In these examples, the speaker highlights the type or category of equipment, disease, care, etc.

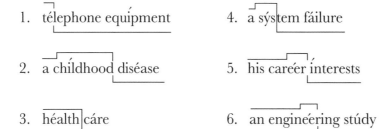

1. télephone equípment
2. a chíldhood diséase
3. héalth|cáre
4. a sýstem fáilure
5. his caréer ínterests
6. an engineéring stúdy

In contrast, when the noun phrase consists of an adjective + noun combination, rising intonation generally occurs on the stressed syllable of the noun. In these examples, the speaker highlights the noun (*equipment, disease, care*), not the adjective that describes it.

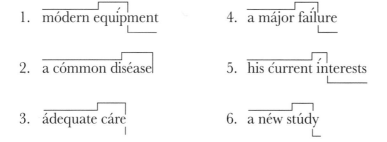

1. módern equípment
2. a cómmon diséase
3. ádequate cáre
4. a májor fáilure
5. his cúrrent ínterests
6. a néw stúdy

In all the examples, notice that the speaker's intonation rises and then falls to low level not mid level because the speaker comes to a full stop. But if the speaker merely pauses slightly, intonation drops to mid level and the speaker continues.

Guidelines for determining which word to highlight in the noun phrase are helpful but do not apply in every case. Compare *computer skills* and *analytical skills.* The noun *computer* functions as an adjective while *analytical* is an adjective, but they are generally pronounced with the same intonation pattern.

This position requires compúter skílls.

This position requires analýtical skílls.

In these examples, the focus appears to be on the types or category of skills required.

Compare, on the other hand, the speaker's use of rising intonation in these two utterances. In the first, even though *computer* is a noun functioning as an adjective, the speaker chooses to focus on *processing* (cf. other types of computer work, such as computer *programming)*. In the second, the speaker focuses on the type of processing, *film* processing (cf. other types of processing, such as *paper* processing).

Today I'll limit my discussion to compúter prócessing.

Today I'd like to continue my discussion on fílm prócessing.

When additional adjectives are added to either of the two patterns, the intonation pattern does not generally change. However, these adjectives tend to convey important information and thus may also be stressed.

He's a résearch assístant. ///   *He is a qúalified résearch assístant. ///*

He's a hígh-lével manàger. ///   *He is a qúalified hígh-level manàger. ///*

It is important to note that, no matter what the general guidelines are, rising intonation can occur on any word that the speaker chooses to highlight.

In this example, the speaker may be reassuring the listener that the speaker correctly understands which is the older equipment (compared to the newer equipment).

That's right. This is the ólder equipment.

Here, a listener may not have heard the final word in the sentence (processing). The speaker may be clarifying.

I said film prócessing.

Task 17: Noun Phrases and Rising Intonation

Listen to your instructor read these sentences. Noun + noun and adjective + noun combinations are in italics. Mark the rising intonation. Which of the words you underlined didn't follow the typical pattern of rising and falling intonation? Why?

1. You want damages for your *medical expenses*.* Damages is compensation for your *financial loss*.

2. One type of injury is *physical injury*.** An example of a *physical injury* is a *head concussion*.

3. Let's go back to the *broken-nose situation*.

4. When you go on *hiking trips*, it's important to take along enough *camping supplies*. One common supply campers are familiar with is *dehydrated food*.

5. A *volcanic eruption* can have *serious consequences*. For example, it can cause *eye and lung problems*.

---

*In this example, the intonation rises on *medical* in the first sentence. This is likely because the speaker wishes to emphasize the type of expenses.

**In this example, the intonation rises on *physical* in the first sentence. Here the speaker may wish to emphasize the type of injury. In the second sentence, the speaker may continue to highlight *physical* but will more likely switch the emphasis to *injury*.

Task 18: Evaluating Your Intonation

Alone or with a partner, practice saying the sentences in Task 17. Then record yourself. Using the space provided, make notes to evaluate your intonation in those places where noun + noun or adjective + noun occur.

Should You Write Your Speech?

Some speakers find it helpful to write their speeches. If you are having trouble organizing material or feel somewhat unsure of how to develop your speech, writing it on a computer can be useful. Once you've written it, you can read through it, get a feel for how well it's developed, and make necessary changes. In addition, your instructor can review it and offer comments before you actually give your presentation. However, remember to write your speech as you would say it, not read it. And don't be tempted to memorize your speech word for word once you have written it. Trying to memorize your speech may cause you to become anxious during your presentation if you forget the exact words you were going to say. Instead, practice once or twice using your script. As you read, try to look up as much as possible. Then practice again and rely only on the visual you've made of the outline of your speech. You may find that writing the first few sentences of your speech and developing a good outline can be just as helpful as writing your entire speech. You will look more natural and be able to maintain eye contact with the audience members.

Task 19: Definition Presentation

Prepare a five- to seven-minute extended-definition presentation of a term from your field of study. Choose a term that you can explain to the members of a general audience.

1. Carefully construct your opening. Before introducing your term, develop an attention-getting opening and provide context for your audience. Ease your listeners into the term and definition.

2. Stress the term you will define. Make sure you pronounce it properly. To guarantee the audience is following, use the term in the title of your visuals and restate or rephrase the definition if necessary.

3. Give a clear, well-constructed one- or two-sentence definition of your term. Choose a three-part definition or use an appropriate alternative from the list on page 110 or in Task 9 on page 109.

4. Develop or extend your definition. Choose a strategy for organizing the type(s) of information you plan to include in your definition. See page 101.

5. Use appropriate connecting devices to move from one part of your speech to another. Try using *let me, okay,* and *so,* as well as *let's.*

6. Use substitutions to quickly clarify any terms in your speech that may be unclear to your audience. Review types of substitutions on page 110.

7. Keep in touch with your audience during the presentation. Use rhetorical or direct questions. At natural breaks in your presentation, ask questions to find out if your audience is following you. Also request questions from the audience. Include the audience members as participants in your presentation when possible.

8. Use visuals to enhance your presentation. It can be advantageous to include your speech outline on a visual. If you think a picture is preferable, choose one that is large and clear with bold lettering (see Unit 2). Or use both an outline and a pictures.

9. Practice your speech at least five or six times. Record yourself twice and evaluate your progress using the evaluation form on pages 130–31. Listen for fillers, hesitations, and pauses. Do they sound natural or do you need more practice? Prepare a note card, if necessary, but don't read or memorize your speech word for word.

Definition Speech Evaluation

Definition Speech Evaluation Form			
Name: _____			
	(Make a check in the appropriate column)		
	Good	OK	Needs Work	Comments (include specific problems you noticed)
Did you use an attention-getting opener?				
Did you place the term in a context before defining it?				
Did you give a well-constructed one-sentence definition of the term?				
Did you pronounce the term correctly?				
Did you say the definition slowly and clearly, emphasizing the key words in the sentence and repeating or rephrasing when necessary?				
Did you extend the definition in a way or ways that made your speech interesting?				
Did you carefully organize information? Explain.				
Did you define other terms as you gave your speech using substitutions, such as synonyms, paraphrases, examples, and acronyms?				
Did you stay in touch with the audience? If so, how?				
Were your visuals clear and easy to read? Was the term included in the title of your first visual?				
Did you display an outline or use some other means of guiding the audience through the presentation?				

	(Make a check in the appropriate column)			
	Good	OK	Needs Work	Comments (include specific problems you noticed)
Did you allow for questions from the audience as you gave your presentation?				
Did you use *Let me* (*Lemme*) or other similar cues to tell the audience what you were going to do next?				
Did you practice enough so that your speech wasn't hesitant and choppy and you didn't overuse fillers?				

Pronunciation

(specific problems)

Other comments

Goals for my next presentation (list 2–3 areas that you want to improve for your next presentation)

Unit 5

Giving a Problem-Solution Speech

In academic environments, instructors and students often discuss problems and how to solve them. Students in Civil Engineering courses talk about problems with building sites, students in Urban Planning debate solutions to urban sprawl, students majoring in Art consider ways to avoid toxic paints or the merits of certain artists, and students in Computer Science courses share ideas for overcoming limitations in current computer hardware. In this unit, you will give a problem-solution speech about a problem in your field.

When giving a problem-solution speech, speakers often organize information according to a four-part structure.

Description of a **situation**	**Situation**
Identification and description of a **problem**	**Problem**
Discussion of one or more **solutions** or **responses** to the problem	**Solution**
Evaluation of the solution(s)	**Evaluation**

In the **situation** section, the speaker provides the necessary background information for understanding the problem and how it has arisen. In the **problem** section, the speaker identifies and discusses the problem. As part of the discussion, the speaker generally explains the reasons for the problem and may also discuss inadequate solutions to the problem. Depending on the nature of the problem, speakers may choose to combine the situation and problem sections. In the **solution** or **response** section, the speaker generally highlights one solution and discusses it in detail. In the **evaluation** section, the speaker evaluates the solution by pointing out its strengths and weaknesses. The last two sections may overlap, depending on how the speaker organizes information.

Two primary reasons to use a problem-solution pattern of organization are to

❏ provide a simple means of ordering and remembering information
❏ help audience members follow the presentation because they will be able to predict how the presentation will develop

132

Some of the speech topics you have already presented can be adapted to conform to a problem-solution structure. For example, a term you have defined, such as toxicity or attention deficit disorder (A.D.D.), might, by its nature, be considered a problem to be solved. A recently designed object or procedure may, on the other hand, be considered a solution to a problem.

Task 1: A Device for the Hearing Impaired

Read the problem-solution speech about a device for hearing impaired people. Identify the different parts (situation, problem, solution, evaluation). Then answer the questions on page 135 with a partner or small group.

Induction Loops

① How many of you have someone in your family who suffers from hearing loss? Data from the National Institute of Deafness and Other Communication Disorders shows that in the United States, more and more people suffer from hearing loss as they age. As you can see in this graph, 18% of people between ages 45 and 64 and 30% of people between ages 65 and 74 experience hearing loss. And almost 50% of people over age 75 are hearing impaired.*

Hearing Impaired in the United States

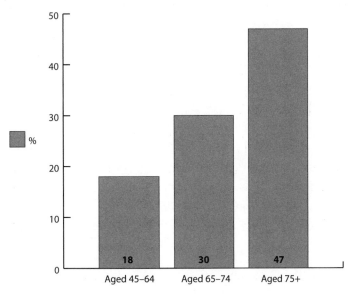

Source: Data from the National Institute of Deafness and Other Communication Disorders, June 16, 2010.

---

* Information from www.nidcd.nih.gov/.

② So you can see that the older you get, the more likely you'll have trouble hearing. But, what about younger people? They may also have hearing loss, especially if they've been exposed to a lot of noise, like listening to loud music, work-related noise, or riding motorcycles.

③ Hearing loss is usually caused by damage to your hair cells in your inner ear. Hair cells change sounds to electrical signals that go to the brain. Once these hair cells are damaged, they don't grow back. So far there is no cure for hearing loss. At this point, hearing aids are the best available option. Better hearing aids have been developed over the years, and they do a good job in quiet settings, but they aren't a perfect solution. People who wear them complain that they amplify background noise, room reverberation, and static. This can be especially annoying in public places like theaters and concert halls, where things like feet shuffling, paper rustling or someone's cough will be picked up by a hearing aid and make it hard to hear and really enjoy an event.

④ Now, however, there's an innovative solution to this problem called an induction loop or a hearing loop. The loop is basically a copper wire that's installed on the floor around the periphery of a room. It can be installed in places like movie houses, lecture rooms, concert houses, and even ticket booths at railway stations, and your TV room at home. What it does is it sends out electromagnetic signals from the microphone or another amplification device to a wireless receiver in the hearing aid called a telecoil or t-coil. Today, most hearing aids come with this wireless receiver. When the hearer activates the t-coil, the microphone in the hearing aid automatically turns off and the t-coil changes the electromagnetic signals coming from the loop to audible sound. For people wearing hearing aids, the sounds come through loud and clear. People who have used the loop say that they are astonished by how clear and rich the sounds are.

⑤ One problem is that loop induction only works when a person is wearing a hearing aid with a t-coil and is in a venue with a microphone or another magnetic source. Another problem is that up-front costs of installing a loop may be expensive, depending on the size of the venue. But only one loop is needed for a large number of people so the relative cost per person can be low. And once a loop is installed, it's not expensive to maintain and no other equipment is necessary.

Discussion Questions

1. In the situation section, how does the speaker raise interest in the topic? Who is the likely audience?

2. Where does the problem section begin? What words are used to announce the beginning of the problem section?

3. What effect might the graph have on the audience?

4. The speaker uses the word *innovative* to introduce the solution. Which of these words could be used instead?

   adequate, clever, creative, convenient, impressive, interesting, proposed, tricky, neat, risky, attractive, simple

5. What process does the speaker describe? (See Unit 3) Is it clear or difficult to understand?

6. Should the speaker include this information at the end of the speech?

   If you aren't hard of hearing but are also bothered by feet shuffling, talking, or paper rattling, you can also get a device that blocks out background noise but doesn't require a hearing aid.

7. Would you use other visuals for this presentation? Explain.

8. What question might you ask the speaker?

The speaker uses a typical problem-solution structure for the speech. The situation section gives data on hearing loss and the use of hearing aids. The speaker involves younger listeners in the opening statement by pointing out that hearing problems aren't limited to the elderly. The speaker then moves on to discuss the main problem—that hearing aids amplify various types of noise.

Then the speaker moves on to the solution section and introduces an *innovative* solution—the loop. The use of *innovative* informs the audience of the speaker's opinion of the solution. Some other adjectives that could be used are *impressive, clever,* or *relatively inexpensive.* In the evaluation section, the speaker addresses issues of cost but does not provide specific costs for installation of an inductive coil or purchase of a hearing aid. The speaker highlights the enthusiasm of those hard-of-hearing individuals who have had a "loop" experience but doesn't provide any survey data. Some questions for the speaker might be:

1. Are there any venues where the cost of installing a coil would be too expensive?
2. Could the hearing-aid wearer use a coil at a picnic?
3. Can people who aren't hard of hearing take advantage of a loop when they go to a concert?

Signaling Problems or Disadvantages

In a problem-solution speech, speakers generally signal to the audience that they are moving from the situation to the problem by means of a connecting device or other signal that announces the problem. There are three common devices that speakers use.

Adversarial words that signal that a situation has created a problem	but, however, although, even though, nevertheless, in spite of + noun Although hearing aids work well in smaller, quiet settings, they . . .
Adverbs that introduce a problem	unfortunately, sadly Unfortunately, hearing aids can be expensive.
Phrases that indicate a problem	The problem is that . . . Younger people are being exposed to louder noise. The problem is caused by background noise, reverberation, and static.

In a problem-solution speech, speakers can signal that they are moving from the problem to the solution using the expression *in order to* + verb or vocabulary such as *one way/solution/method/approach/*. Speakers can also use a rhetorical question, such as *So, what is a workable solution to this problem?*

Signaling a Solution

In a problem-solution speech, speakers move from the problem to the solution by using a signal that announces the solution. The following are common ways to introduce a solution in English. Notice that all of them contain an infinitive (*to* + verb).

Strategy	Example
A purpose statement using the infinitive (*in order*) *to* + verb	**(In order) to address** the problem of obesity in young people, *school menus are being modified.*
The expression *one way* + *to* verb	**One way to provide** *medical care to people in remote rural areas is by television.*
The expression *one solution /approach to the problem is to* + verb (or verb + *-ing*)	**One solution to the problem** of rising tuition costs **is to give** *more scholarships.*

Referring to Graphs

In discussing problems and solutions, it can be helpful to illustrate information using tables, graphs, charts, and other visuals such as drawings or photos. In the presentation on the induction loop, the speaker uses a graph to compare hearing loss in three different populations based on age. The speaker first introduces the graph by using a common expression, *As you can see from this graph*. There are many ways to introduce a graph.

> *This graph compares hearing loss among three different age groups.*
>
> *As shown in the graph . . . .*
>
> *Here in this graph you can see that . . . .*
>
> *(Let's) take a look at this graph.*

In addition, the speaker summarizes the survey findings by saying, *So you can see that the older you get, the more likely you'll have trouble hearing.* The speaker could also have begun by first summarizing the findings and then presenting specific details about each age group.

Task 2: Explaining Graphs

Working with a partner or small group, look at the four graphs and talk about how you would introduce them. Also decide what you would say about each of the graphs. What do they reveal? What general statement would you make about the information? Would you introduce the data before or after this statement? Practice presenting one of the graphs. In which part of a problem-solution speech might they be discussed?

Garbage Produced per Person in the United States

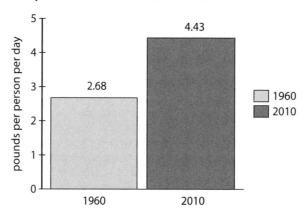

Source: Data from United States Environmental Protection Agency www.epa.gov/epawaste/nonhaz/municipal/index.htm, November 2012.

Percentage of Garbage Recycled in the United States

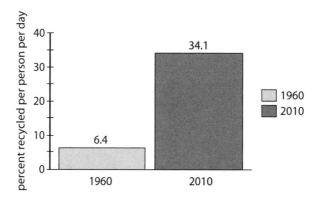

Source: Data from United States Environmental Protection Agency www.epa.gov/epawaste/nonhaz/municipal/index.htm, November 2012.

Tuition, Room, Board, U.S. Higher Education, 2010–2011

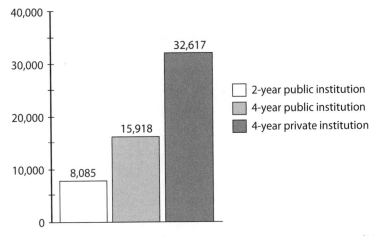

- ☐ 2-year public institution
- 4-year public institution
- 4-year private institution

Source: National Center for Education Statistics, www.nces.ed.gov/fastfacts/display.asp?id+76.

U.S. Crimes, Crime Rates by Type of Offense, 1980 and 2009

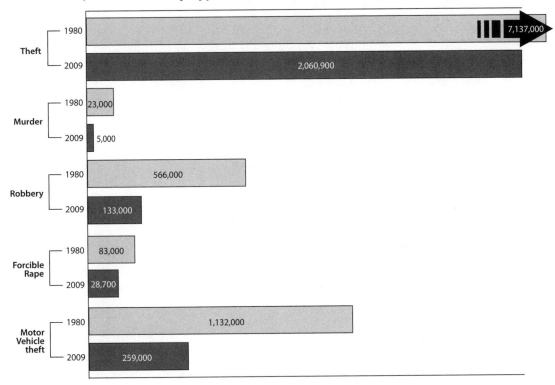

Source: U.S. Department of Justice, Federal Bureau of Investigation, "Crime in the United States," September 2010, www2.fbi.gov/ucr/cius2009/index.html; www.census.gov/compendia/statab/2012/tables/12s0306.pdf

Organizing Information

Task 3: Controlling an Invasive Species

Read this problem-solution speech. Mark the situation, problem, solution(s), and evaluation sections. Then answer the questions.

1. In Sections 2–4, how does the speaker organize information?
2. How does the speaker begin Sections 2–4?

Purple Loosestrife

① You might have seen a tall, bright purple plant growing along some of the rivers and lakes in this area. This attractive plant is called purple loosestrife. It's a wetland species from Europe and Asia that was brought to the United States in the 1800s. It spread quickly and unfortunately has had a devastating effect on thousands of areas of wetland across the U.S. and Canada.

② Here are some reasons why. First, it multiplies quickly because it reproduces quickly—one adult plant can disperse more than two million seeds annually. Second, it doesn't have any natural enemies in North America, so it forces out native vegetation that provides food for many wetland wildlife species. And third, it's made up of really dense strands, which means that it can't be used as cover or nesting sites for many wetland animals such as ducks, frogs, and turtles.

③ The following typical plant control methods have been tried with little success. Burning. Burning doesn't control plant roots, seeds or seedling plants. Mowing. Mowing can lead to uncontrolled growth because the plant's roots and broken stems can resprout. And herbicides. These are expensive and tend to kill native vegetation, giving loosestrife an opportunity to take over their site.

④ Today two main solutions are used to address the problem. One is introducing several kinds of beetles from Europe. These insects eat various parts of the loosestrife plant, including the flower and foliage. They have several advantages. First, they feed only on loosestrife. In addition, once they become established they should be able to provide year-round control of the plant. Furthermore, they're inexpensive. The other solution involves volunteers who physically remove loosestrife from areas where it grows and then re-introduce native plants. This requires community involvement and can be time consuming.

⑤ Both methods have been successful in reducing the problem and controlling the spread of loosestrife.

Listing

In the Purple Loosestrife speech, the speaker makes use of listing strategies to organize information: He lists (1) three reasons that loosestrife has had a serious effect on public wetlands; (2) two reasons that loosestrife multiplies quickly; (3) three unsuccessful solutions to the problem; and (4) two solutions to the problem and three advantages to the first solution. Listing is a simple and frequently used organizational pattern in academic speaking.

Listing is often incorporated into a broader organizational pattern, such as problem-solution. Common listing devices include:

- ❐ Enumerators–ordinal numbers*
  - *first*
  - *second*
  - *third*
- ❐ Other listing connectors or additives,** such as
  - *furthermore*
  - *in addition*
  - *moreover*
  - *what's more*
  - *also*
  - *plus*
  - *besides*
  - *finally*
  - *and last*
  - *one clever solution is . . . another is . . .*
  - *the most dangerous problem is . . . others include . . .*

---

*Notice that *at first* isn't in this list. It is used to mean "originally" or "in the beginning." It is generally followed by *but then* to indicate a change (e.g., in belief, opinion, situation, plan). For example: *At first, it seemed loosestrife was harmless, but then environmentalists noticed it was pushing out native plants.*

**Notice that *at last* isn't on this list. *Finally* and *last* can be used as additives, but *at last* cannot. *At last* means "after a long time." For example: *At last, scientists have found a way to control loosestrife.*

❏   Gerunds, noun phrases, imperatives, or other expressions that summarize the elements or items in the list.

- Burning: *Burning doesn't control plant roots, seeds, or seedling plants.*
- Mowing: *Mowing can lead to uncontrolled growth.*
- *Pull out the plants by hand.*
- *Re-introduce native plants.*

In the first two examples, the speaker effectively highlights the topic of the sentence before saying the whole sentence.

❏   A bullet strategy using cardinal numbers

This solution has these advantages:
- *One, it's inexpensive.*
- *Two, it's readily available.*
- *And three, it's been proven effective.*

This method is fast-paced and effective for presenting short lists.

❏   A bullet strategy with no listing connectors

This solution has these advantages:
- *It's inexpensive.*
- *It's readily available.*
- *It's effective.*

In this strategy, the speaker simply presents the contents of the list without using enumerators or other listing strategies. This method is quick-paced and direct. It can be effective when presenting short lists.

Speaking to Persuade: Providing Evidence

In academic speaking, one of the goals for presenters may be to persuade listeners to their position on a given topic. Much persuasive academic discourse centers around problems and solutions. For example, business and economics students may be expected to convince the audience that a company is facing an impending financial crisis. In other words, they must persuade the audience that there is a problem. Educators may be asked to justify their curriculum design, or psychologists to defend their choice of a treatment plan. In other words, they may be expected to defend their solution to a perceived problem.

The ability to persuade depends in part on the supporting evidence we provide. However, members of different academic communities use different persuasive strategies. In some fields, stories and other anecdotal evidence may be convincing, while in others statistical data may be highly regarded. Persuasive evidence is generally defined by the members of a particular discipline. Even then, not everyone in that discipline may agree.

Task 4: Types of Evidence

Different types of evidence may be needed at different stages of the problem-solution speech. In your field of studies, what types of evidence are generally used to show that there is a problem? What types of evidence are used to evaluate a particular solution?

Evidence	To Indicate a Problem	To Evaluate a Solution
1. Results of research studies/tests		
2. Questionnaires, surveys, and other collected data		
3. General knowledge, facts		
4. Observations, observations over time		
5. Description of symptoms, feelings		
6. Anecdotal or experiential evidence		
7. Physical evidence or pictures		
8. Other (write in type):		
9. Other (write in type):		

Task 5: Evaluating Evidence

Read the nine excerpts and discuss with a partner what types of evidence the speakers used to make their case for (1) the existence of a problem or (2) a viable solution. Refer to the list in Task 4. Evaluate the evidence in each. What further evidence or information should the speaker provide?

1. One woman who walks to work on rubber sidewalks says that she definitely notices the difference. They have a softer surface than cement sidewalks.

2. Rubber sidewalks, which are made from recycled tires, cost about 60 percent more than cement sidewalks but are cost effective, especially when used around trees. As you've probably noticed, cement sidewalks are often damaged by tree roots and have to be broken up and replaced. Rubber sidewalks last much longer because they can be picked up to cut tree roots away, and then repositioned.

3. A study organized by the Center for Science in the Public Interest concluded that 85 percent of snacks in school vending machines had poor nutritional value.

4. When my grandmother attended a four-year private college in the 1960s, the cost of tuition, room, and board was around $2,100. Today at that same private college, the cost of tuition, room, and board is more than $43,000.

5. A large portion of the population in India still lives in rural areas. Because doctors there now are able to consult with specialists in larger hospitals via television, hundreds of patients have been successfully treated in local community hospitals.

6. Recent tests showed that only about 35 percent of eighth graders in the U.S. are proficient in math.

7. One study using high-quality testing procedures showed that the number of adolescents with some degree of hearing loss increased more than 30 percent over a period of approximately 15 years.

8. Until now, scientists had been unable to prove that bears were capable of using tools. Recently, however, photos taken of a bear show it using a rock as a tool.

9. Many large shopping malls have closed over the last decade because of a drop in sales. Reis, Inc., a New York research firm, reports that the vacancy rate rose last year to more than 9 percent.

Anticipating Questions from the Audience

As you discuss the problem you have raised and the solution you offer, audience members may raise questions about (1) the legitimacy of your problem and (2) the efficacy of your solution. You may be able to anticipate these questions and be prepared to provide additional data in your speech or in response to questions.

For example, in Task 5, Speakers 1–3 might prepare answers to these questions before their presentations.

- ❏ How much more wear-and-tear on the body do cement sidewalks actually contribute than rubber?
- ❏ Even though rubber sidewalks last much longer, they have to be maintained. How much would that cost compared to replacing cement sidewalks?
- ❏ How does the study define "poor nutritional value"?

What questions would you ask Speakers 4, 5, and 6?

Task 6: Two Types of Questions

Some members of the audience may ask questions for information, while others may ask questions that attempt to challenge to the speaker's position. The intent of the listener is not always clear. Look at the questions. Which seem to be a request for additional information (I), and which may be an attempt by the listener to highlight a possible weakness (W) in the speaker's position? Explain. If you were the speaker, what would you say if you didn't know the answer to the question?

_____ 1. Won't these imported beetles take a liking to some native, non-invasive loosestrife plants in the U.S. and destroy them?

_____ 2. Are there estimates on how many acres of loosestrife these beetles have eliminated?

_____ 3. Can't beetles brought from abroad carry parasites?

_____ 4. Wouldn't pulling out loosestrife by hand be time-consuming? Do you know how long it takes? How reliable is this method?

_____ 5. I'm wondering what percentage of people can't take advantages of hearing loops because they can't afford a hearing aid? How much would a hearing aid typically cost?

_____ 6. What can people do who have hearing aids that don't have a t-coil?

_____ 7. Induction loops seem to be a rather simple solution to a big problem. Why did it take so long for loops to become widespread?

Notice the use of the negative question forms in Questions 1, 3, and 4. Listeners that incorporate negative question forms (_can't, shouldn't, isn't it possible, don't you think_) may indicate that they are questioning the speaker's claim(s).

Ways to Critique a Solution

Both the speaker and audience members may wish to point out advantages and disadvantages to a proposed solution.

Advantages	Disadvantages
Show that the solution	Show that the solution
• Solves the problem or accomplishes objectives (objectives effectively match outcome)	• Is not supported by data
• Controls or reduces a specific problem	• Is supported by insufficient or unreliable data
• Does not create new problems (or they are minimal)	• Doesn't totally address the problem
• Sometimes leads to unexpected benefits	• Doesn't accomplish objectives
• Produces abstract benefits, such as fairness	• Is ineffective
• Accomplishes long-lasting results	• Is of limited benefit, isn't bold enough
• Promises better results in the future	• Creates adverse effects or negative consequences, worsens the problem, or causes it to spread
• Has fewer side effects, negative effects or impact	• Overlooks the real causes of the problem
• Creates positive responses, minimizes negative responses	• Minimizes the problem
• Curbs negative behavior, encourages positive behavior	• Views the problem too narrowly or too broadly
• Can be broadly applied, has more benefits for more people	• Fosters poor quality
• Can be narrowly applied, benefits a target group	
	Is
Addresses specific issues of	simplistic
durability	inefficient
strength	complex
efficiency	costly
cost	short-lived
stability	unsafe, risky
accessibility	inaccurate
quality	inaccessible
accuracy	weak
aesthetics	unattractive to the eye
safety	out-of-date
comfort	other _____
pleasure	other _____
other _____	
other _____	

Evaluating Your Solution

Your problem-solution presentation may trigger audience skepticism if you don't provide enough evidence to show that the problem has merit or that there is sufficient benefit to the solution.

During the evaluation section, you may also open yourself to criticism if you fail to make a fair appraisal of your own solution – in other words, to give your solution a positive evaluation while acknowledging any weaknesses.

For example, you can point out that the disadvantages to your solution

- ❏ are minor or easily overcome
- ❏ are less serious than disadvantages of other solutions
- ❏ will likely be reduced over time
- ❏ will be addressed by plans for further research

These hedging strategies allow you to discuss limitations to your solution while still expressing confidence in it. They also provide an opportunity to suggest future research or data collection.

Task 7: Hedging Strategies

Look at the statements made by speakers in their evaluation section. Underline the hedging strategy(ies) that the speakers use in their conclusions. How could you weaken or strengthen these conclusions?

1. Even though they're cost-effective, some smaller venues may need time to raise additional funds to install induction loops.

2. So far, evidence seems to show that European beetles feed exclusively on invasive loosestrife and do not appear to damage other plants.

3. Providing nutritional information on healthy food in schools can somewhat improve children's eating habits at home.

4. Beetles should be able to provide year-round protection against loosestrife unless their numbers are greatly reduced by predators. Currently there is no evidence that this is taking place.

5. If the government provides funding for hearing aids for the elderly poor, they will be able to take advantage of venues where hearing loops are installed.

6. The trend to convert malls to mixed-use areas will receive the support of the much of the business community in malls where the number of shoppers is declining.

7. We can conclude from our pilot study that many older community college students who work full-time are often more successful than their younger classmates.

Ways to Qualify Your Claims

Among the many ways you can hedge or qualify your claims in English are to use

- ❑ modals (*may, should, could, might not*)
- ❑ adverbs (*normally, often, sometimes, rarely, likely, somewhat*)
- ❑ adjectives (*some, most, almost all*)
- ❑ numbers and percentages (*a small number of, only two, 50% of our subjects*)
- ❑ conditionals (*if, unless*)
- ❑ prepositional phrases (*in the short term, under these circumstances, in this geographical area, under the age of 50, even though they are readily available*)
- ❑ time expressions (*so far, until now, currently*)
- ❑ verbs (*appear, seem, suggest, show, indicate*)

Task 8: Using a Speech Outline

After designing the first draft of his purple loosestrife speech, the speaker decides to include an additional paragraph after his introduction. Read the new paragraph. Then, with a partner, answer the questions.

① You might have seen a tall, bright purple plant growing along some of the rivers and lakes in this area. This attractive plant is called purple loosestrife. It's a wetland species from Europe and Asia that was brought to the United States in the 1800s. It spread quickly and unfortunately has had a devastating effect on thousands of areas of across the U.S. and Canada.

② Today I'm going to explain why purple loosestrife has become a problem and what is being done to solve it. First I'll discuss the reasons that loosestrife has had a serious impact on public wetlands in the United States. Then I'll outline some of the methods that have been unsuccessfully used to control loosestrife. And finally, I'll introduce a unique way to control loosestrife that appears to be both safe and effective. All right, let's take a look at why loosestrife has had such a devastating effect on these areas. First, loosestrife multiplies quickly.

Discussion Questions

1. What is the purpose of the first sentence in the overview?

2. After introducing his topic, the speaker inserts an overview or outline summary. What is its purpose?

3. What connecting devices does the speaker use in his overview?

4. What modal does he use?

5. How does the speaker "get back" to his speech? In other words, after he finishes his overview, how does he make the transition to the problem section?

6. In the overview, the speaker doesn't tell the audience what solution he is going to present? Why not?

Providing an Overview or Outline Summary

An overview or outline summary provides a brief outline of the speech to the audience. In a typical overview, the speaker tells the audience what information to listen for and how it will be organized but doesn't generally give specific content information. An overview generally contains a one-sentence statement summarizing the speech topic. It's followed by a brief summary of each section of the speech. Speakers use time connectors, such as *first, then, after that,* and *finally* to indicate the order in which they will proceed. They also typically use *I'm going to* or the modal *will (I'll)* in each section of the overview. Speakers may provide an overview because

❐ their speech is long.

❐ their audience is unfamiliar with the topic.

❐ they want to acquaint the audience with their organizational strategy.

In order avoid confusion, speakers who use an overview generally don't stray or deviate from it during their speech.*

Task 9: Evaluating Questions from the Audience

It is not always necessary to respond to every question a member of the audience asks. Imagine that you are the speaker in these situations. How will you reply if

- you are going to answer the listener's question in the next part of the speech.

- the question is too long to answer given the time constraints.

- the question would cause you to digress too much from your topic.

---

*If speakers wish to digress from their planned speech, it is helpful if they announce the digression (e.g., *Let me digress for a minute*).

Task 10: Preparing for Questions from the Audience

After preparing your speech, write a list of questions that you think you should be prepared to answer about a speech you gave in Unit 4. Then practice giving your answers to the questions.

1.

2.

3.

4.

Additional Tips for Answering Questions from the Audience

> Answer the specific question that was asked.

> Make your answer short (summarize it) so that you will have time for other questions and will not tire the audience.

> Try to organize your answer.

> If you don't know the answer, don't pretend that you do. If appropriate, refer the audience to sources of information.

> Restate the question in case the audience may not have heard it.

> Reword the question in case the audience may not have understood it.

Task 11: An Alternative to Driving

Read this problem-solution speech and then, with a partner, answer the questions on page 155.

Driverless Cars

① When you're driving to work or school, do you ever get the urge to send a text message, even though you know it's against the law? What about driving on long trips? After 5 or 6 hours, do you usually start feeling that you're not as sharp as when you started out? Or, when you're driving, do you worry about your driving record? Have you gotten many expensive speeding tickets? If you get another one, will you lose your license? Or, are you just a nervous driver who doesn't like to drive?

② Soon there'll a solution to all these problems—a driverless car. Actually, driverless cars, which are also called autonomous or self-driving cars, are already allowed on the road in three states— Florida, Nevada, and California. And, in California, they've driven well over 300,000 miles, and 60,000 miles with no human intervention. A lot of Californians may not realize they're driving next to a driverless car because driverless cars are currently required to have a passenger behind the steering wheel. So, strange as it may seem, soon it looks like you can get some driving help from a robot, who can take you where you want to go.

③ How do these cars work? Driverless cars use several different kinds of technologies—radar sensors, video cameras, computers, laser scanners, artificial-intelligence software. These features enable them to do such tasks as read physical signs, receive electronic road signals, watch out for things in the way, and navigate by identifying paths. They get information from their surroundings, such as from other cars. They can even update path information.

④ Here are some commonly asked questions and their answers about driverless cars.

Question 1. Isn't it more dangerous to be in a driverless car than being in control yourself? (*pause*)

In California, none of these cars has caused an accident. They're safer because they eliminate human error, which causes most accidents. And for you, this can result in lower auto insurance rates and fewer traffic tickets. It also means savings for the police department because it can cut back on the number of traffic police.

Question 2. Could people who are blind or who can't see very well get around without a driver? (*pause*)

Currently, people still need a license to drive, but someday they probably won't.

Question 3. Wouldn't driverless cars have to wait in traffic as much as we do? (*pause*)

They actually handle traffic flow problems better than humans. And this, along with other factors, can make them more fuel-efficient.

Question 4. What if you wanted or needed to take back control from your car? (*pause*)

If drivers sitting behind the wheel want to take over from their robot, all they have to do is perform a simple action like stepping on the brake.

Question 5. What about the expense of getting a car with all these gadgets? (*pause*)

Right now, self-driving cars are very expensive and most of us can't afford one. But in the future, even if they cost more than the car you have right now, you'll likely be able to save money over the long run with less fuel consumption, insurance premiums, and hopefully no more traffic tickets.

⑤ People have raised some valid questions about driverless cars. The first is about privacy. What kinds of information can your car track about you that can be used by someone else? The second has to do with liability. If self-driving cars cause an accident, who would get the ticket? The third has to do with break-downs. What if one of the gadgets on the car stops working? What happens? If someone is sitting behind the wheel, what would the reaction time have to be?

⑥ Some of you may be skeptical about driverless cars. But keep in mind that people were skeptical about electricity when it was first invented. As for me, I'm looking forward to the day when my car will be able to drop me off at the airport and then drive itself home.

⑦ Soon you'll be free to get some work done in your car, send a few text messages, do the crossword puzzle, maybe even take a nap. Or you may choose to just sit back and enjoy the ride.

Discussion Questions

1. Does this speech follow the situation-problem-solution-evaluation pattern? Explain.

2. What strategy does the speaker use in the problem section of her presentation? Who might the audience be?

3. What information is included in the solution section of the speech? What evidence does the speaker give to convince audience members that they may own a driverless car one day?

4. The speaker asks and answers a series of five questions. Why? Why doesn't the speaker have the audience ask questions at this point?

5. In discussing the answers to the five questions, what hedging strategies does the speaker use?

6. If the speaker were addressing an audience in the fields of Computer Science or Engineering, how might she adjust this presentation? Would the speaker use a visual? If so, what kind?

7. Why does the speaker list some valid concerns about driverless cars?

8. Are you as enthusiastic about driverless cars as the speaker?

The speaker begins by discussing typical problems drivers face in their cars. Audience members may easily relate to one or more of them. Then the speaker offers a solution that addresses all of these problems—driverless cars. The speaker wants to convince the audience that this is a viable solution by pointing out that driverless cars are already on the road. Then the speaker gives some details about how these cars work and what types of tasks they accomplish. This section is meant for non-specialists. The speaker would likely develop a more technical discussion for audience members in computer science and engineering. Both specialists and non-specialists might be interested in seeing a visual with the features discussed in this section.

The speaker then asks and answers questions. This strategy allows the speaker to (1) elaborate on the benefits of driverless cars and (2) anticipate questions from the audience and criticism from skeptics. In the evaluation section, the speaker highlights three concerns that have been raised about driverless cars. The speaker closes by expressing optimism for this new technology.

Pronunciation

Unstressed Words and Syllables

Unstressed Words

The pronunciation sections in Units 2 and 4 discussed stress. Incorrect use of stress may interfere with the audience's ability to understand the speaker. Unit 2 discussed the importance of emphasizing key words. However, it is also important to leave less important words that carry little information unstressed. Since these words are not stressed, they are said quickly.

Say these sentences.

1. Lét's lóok at an exámple.

2. It's a mistáke in the design.

In the first sentence, *let's*, *look*, and *example* are stressed, while *at* and *an* are left unstressed and therefore said quickly. Likewise, in Sentence 2, *mistake* and *design* are stressed, while *it's*, *a*, *in*, and *the* are unstressed.

If we say the words *at* and *an* individually, we stress them. When they are stressed, they have the same vowel sound as *cat* and *hat*. If they are not stressed, however, they are pronounced differently, with an unstressed vowel sound. In English, the two most common are /ɪ/ as in *it*, and the schwa /ə/ as in *us*. In the case of unstressed *at* and *an* in the examples on page 156, the speaker could use /ɪ/. So, *Let's look at an example* would actually sound more like *Let's look it in example*.

In the second sentence, *It's a mistake in the design*, the words *a* and *the* are generally pronounced as the schwa /ə/, whether they are stressed or not.* The schwa is a short vowel sound in which the tongue is relaxed in middle of the mouth. The filler *uh* is pronounced as /ə/.

Task 12: Unstressed Words

Pronounce these sentences. Stress the key words but not the less important words such as *it, is, a, the, at, in, on, of.*

1. Carolína's from the cápital of Cósta Ríca.

2. Wáter móves to the túrbine.

3. The hárp is a músical ínstrument.

4. Lét's lóok at a pícture of the éye.

5. Tuítion is going úp at univérsities in the Únited Státes.

6. Dó thís stép at a quíck páce.

---

*When some speakers stress *a*, they rhyme it with *day* or *say*. When they stress *the* or say it before a word beginning with a vowel (see Sentence 4 in Task 12), they often rhyme it with *tree* or *three*.

Unstressed Syllables of Stressed Words

As was pointed out in Unit 2, key words, when stressed, are usually only stressed heavily on one or two syllables of the word. Other syllables are often pronounced with an unstressed vowel sound. Again, two vowel sounds in English that can function as unstressed vowel sounds are /ɪ/ and /ə/. Take a look at the common words in English listed in Task 13. The vowels in the syllables, marked with ⌣, are pronounced with either /ɪ/ or /ə/. Because the two sounds are very similar, sometimes one or the other may be used, depending on the dialect, the speed at which the word is pronounced, the surrounding sounds and the individual speaker. These unstressed syllables are pronounced quickly. In some words, they may actually disappear. For example, in some dialects of English, the word *dialect* when spoken quickly may be pronounced *di | lect* rather than *di | a | lect*.

Task 13: Syllables with Unstressed Vowel Sounds

Practice saying these words, using one of these unstressed syllables where indicated.

reason	reas⌣n
concern	c⌣ncern
product	prod⌣ct
exam	⌣xam
damage	dam⌣ge
engineer	eng⌣neer
microphone	micr⌣phone
symptom	sympt⌣m
production	pr⌣duct⌣n*
president	pres⌣dent
develop	d⌣vel⌣p
introduce	intr⌣duce
mistake	m⌣stake
design	d⌣sign
universe	un⌣verse

*-*tion* in English is commonly pronounced shən/šən/ or zhən /žən/.

degree	d⌣gree
conduction	c⌣nduct⌣n*
conclusion	c⌣nclus⌣n*
solution	s⌣lution
disease	d⌣sease
United States	Unit⌣d States
England	Engl⌣nd
Canada	Can⌣d⌣

Task 14: Academic Words and Phrases

Write some words and phrases used frequently in your field of study. Say them aloud, recording them if possible. Listen to see if you used unstressed vowel sounds /ɪ/ and /ə/ in the unstressed words and syllables that don't receive heavy or primary stress.

*-*tion* in English is commonly pronounced shən/šən/ or zhən /žən/.

Task 15: Problem-Solution Presentation

Prepare a six- to eight-minute presentation on a problem and solution in your field of study using a problem-solution structure to organize your speech. Use these guidelines for your presentation.

1. Choose a topic from your field that will interest a general academic audience. As you prepare your speech, keep in mind that your time is limited. After you practice your speech, you may realize that it is too long. Prioritize information. Decide what information is essential and what can be eliminated.

2. Choose an attention-getting opening.

3. Decide what background information you should include in the situation section of your presentation.

4. Provide an overview of your speech if you think it will benefit the audience. If you add an overview, decide how you will design your visual(s) to accommodate the overview.

5. Decide what strategy you will use to lead up to your problem. Clearly explain the problem and the reasons for it. Provide evidence that the problem exists. Decide whether or not to critique other possible solutions. If you do, use evidence to support your claims. Refer to the list that follows these questions for possible ways to critique a solution.

6. Decide how you will introduce your solution. Explain and evaluate the solution, using evidence for your claims. Highlight advantages and minimize disadvantages where possible. Refer to the box on page 147 for possible ways to critique a solution.

7. Where possible, use listing strategies discussed in the unit.

8. Design a conclusion for your speech.

9. Maintain audience attention. Check for understanding. Encourage listeners to ask questions. Anticipate and prepare for questions and challenges from the audience.

10. Practice your speech five to six times out loud. If your pace is slow and you have a lot of hesitations in certain parts of your presentation, practice those parts again. Evaluate the effectiveness of your presentation by using the form on page 161.

Problem-Solution Speech Evaluation

Problem-Solution Speech Evaluation Form		
Name: _____		
	Yes/No	Comments
Was your topic narrow enough to handle in the time allotted?		
Was your audience interested in your topic? What strategies did you use to build interest at the beginning of your speech?		
Did you adequately signal to the audience the parts of your problem-solution presentation?		
Did you highlight one problem? If there are other problems, did you mention that there are other problems, but you will focus on only one?		
In your speech, did you explain the precise nature of (or reasons for) the problem and provide evidence of the problem?		
In your speech, did you highlight one solution? If there are other solutions, did you choose one to focus on?		
Did you include enough evidence of the success of your solution?		
Did your evaluation allow your audience to understand the potential strengths or weaknesses of the solution?		
Did you use visuals such as graphs or charts to illustrate data?		
Did you use enumerators and other listing strategies where appropriate?		
Did you interact with the audience?		
Did you prepare for questions from the audience?		
Other comments:		

Unit 6 ──

Putting It All Together

Units 1–5 introduced different types of speeches commonly used in an academic setting. Along with these speech types, common organizational patterns and accompanying connecting devices were introduced and discussed. This unit provides opportunities for students to incorporate what they have learned in prior units into other types of academic presentations. The focus of the first part of Unit 6 is on presenting biographical information about well-known and sometimes controversial figures and their impact on their field and beyond. The second part is on presenting research.

Part 1: Presenting Biographical Information

In Unit 1, you introduced another student to the rest of the class. The first section of this unit prepares you to present biographical information about a well-known person in your field of study, such as a modern architect, a British historian, a Nobel Prize–winning economist, a nineteenth-century writer, or a famous scientist or engineer. This biographical sketch may be part of a longer talk you plan to give.

Your goal might be simply to provide background information about the person, such as when and where he or she was born, studied, or worked, as a means of placing the person in a larger historical context. Another goal may be to heighten interest in the person's particular research area, his or her artistic or literary impact, or his or her product or theoretical perspective. A third goal might be to delve into background information about someone to discover how the person's point of view or expertise developed, what controversies surrounded the person, and/or how his or her writings should be interpreted in a larger context.

Task 1: Biographical Information about Two Famous People

Read the excerpts discussing a famous person of historical significance as part of an academic presentation. Then, with a partner, answer the questions on page 165.

1. JAPANESE LITERATURE—UEDA AKINARI*

Ueda Akinari is a very interesting writer. He lived from 1734 to 1809. Akinari was preoccupied with the supernatural—with foxes, badgers, and snakes and evil spirits and ghosts. And he really believed in these things. For Ueda Akinari, this was serious business. This was part of the real world, the world that we live in. It was very much possible to be deceived by a fox or by a badger, or to have a snake fall in love with you and love you to death, drive you to death.

Akinari was born in Osaka. He was the illegitimate child of a prostitute, but when his mother died when he was three years old, he was adopted by a very prosperous family in Osaka. He became interested in literature from when he was young. He published his first book of poetry, *Hai Tai,* when he was twenty-one years old. And when he was in his twenties, he came to be an avid reader of colloquial Chinese fiction. A lot of the stories that he read were ghost stories. These were things that he was interested in. He started writing his own work, his own fiction, when he entered his thirties. His first work of fiction he wrote when he was thirty-two years old . . . .

*From MICASE, with minor modifications.

2. EVOLUTION—CHARLES DARWIN*

Charles Robert Darwin. And I have a few pictures of him. I wanted to show you a young picture of him is because he started doing things when he was twenty-two. Just a few things about him. He was born in Shrewsbury, England, to a well-known and wealthy English family of physicians who just expected that he would go to medical school and continue in the family way, but he dropped out after only two years of medical school because he couldn't stomach the crude surgical practices that were going on at the time, like surgery on children without anesthesia. So he went to divinity school, and he came out as a clergyman by 1831. But mostly what he was doing during this time when he wasn't in classes was he was walking around and collecting specimens and pressing plants, and talking to animals. He just was a naturalist at heart.

After Darwin got out of college, he got this great job offer to join the crew of this survey ship called the *H-M-S Beagle*. He was hired on as the crew's naturalist. He was already a really good naturalist. His knowledge of natural history and geology probably surpassed most of his contemporaries even though he was just twenty-two. And they set off on a five-year voyage . . . .

---

*From MICASE, with minor modifications.

Discussion Questions

1. What information do the speakers give that heightens your interest in Ueda Akinari and Charles Darwin? What do Akinari and Darwin have in common?

2. Why do you think the speakers each gave biographical information about their personal lives in an academic discussion?

3. What organizational style predominates in these two passages?

4. Which of the two people likely sparked more controversy in his lifetime?

5. What do you think the first speaker will discuss next? The second speaker?

6. What are some examples of the casual style used by these speakers?

Task 2: Well-Known People and Their Work

Read the passages, each of which references a well-known person. Then, with a partner, answer the questions on page 167.

1. ART—THOMAS COURTURE*

The French artist, Thomas Courture, is an interesting transitional figure because as a teacher, he shaped a generation of artists including Manet. He was able to pass on some new ideas about art that didn't have to do with the classicizing of the past. In Courture's confrontation with artistic traditions, in his effort to be an artist of his own time, what does he do? He abandons the classical past in order to focus on the real, on scenes in the present. He abandons um the fine techni academic artists for something that looks crude. He chall making disturbing art. And he challenges um aesthe time by taking from unusual sources, like imita folk woodcuts.

**From MICASE, with minor modifications.

2. ARCHITECTURE—MAYA LIN

In 1981, a young American woman from Ohio named Maya Lin became a controversial figure overnight. She was an architecture student at Yale University and only 21 years old. Along with more than 1,400 other competitors, she'd submitted her design for the Vietnam Veterans Memorial in Washington, DC. Since the entries were by number and not by name, nothing was known about her. She won the competition and became the first woman and the first person of Chinese descent to design a national memorial in the Mall in Washington, DC. Controversy soon erupted over her heritage and the wall itself. It was an unconventional design for a war memorial. It was a black granite wall set in the earth listing more than 58,000 names in chronological order of those who died in the war. It wasn't done in white granite. It wasn't a statue. There was no American flag or even mention of the Vietnam War. A group of veterans pushed for changes to the memorial, but Lin resisted. To stem the controversy, it was decided to place a traditional sculpture at a distance from the memorial. Today, Maya Lin's wall receives nearly three million visitors a year.

...D HUMAN EVOLUTION—ERNST MAYER*

' Ernst Mayr is most famous for his model of how be...cies) occurs. What he argues is that you differe... that gets isolated from the rest of rest of the species range, species, that gets ...ds with the rest of ...ences between rest of the species ...opulation is in a ...h pressure . . . .

*From MICASE, w...

—**Discussion Questions**————————————————

1. How do these excerpts differ from those in Task 1? What is their focus?

2. Would you call all three people controversial figures? Explain.

3. What tense dominates in Passage 1? Why?

4. What more would you like to know about Maya Lin and her design of the Vietnam Veterans Memorial?

5. Which of these people would you like to meet? Why?

Controversies among Scholars

A person's background, interests, and experiences may form the basis for new models, theories, inventions, cures, discoveries, and artistic and literary expressions. Divergent positions lead to controversies, as can be inferred from the excerpts in Task 2. During your academic studies, you will likely participate in similar controversies in your own fields of study. Tasks 3 and 4 provide practice handling controversies.

Task 3: Polio and the Salk and Sabin Vaccines

Read the presentation.* Then, with a partner, answer the questions on page 169.

Polio Vaccines

① Before the polio vaccine was invented, there was a world-wide epidemic of poliomyelitis. Both Jonas Salk and Albert Sabin were famous for having developed polio vaccines. Salk developed an inactivated or killed polio vaccine, which proved to be successful during trials in the 1950s. Sabin developed a live oral vaccine, which was approved for use in 1961. Salk and Sabin each argued for the widespread use of their own vaccine. The battle went on for many years.

② Sabin believed that only live viruses would be 100 percent effective. The American Medical Association (AMA) took Sabin's position. Salk, however, disagreed and pointed to proof that his vaccine had been effective but that the American Medical Association hadn't carried out mass distribution. Sabin also argued that his vaccine was cheaper and easier to administer because it was given orally on a sugar cube. And, he claimed that because Salk's vaccine had to be injected, children would resist getting it. Salk countered by saying that all other childhood immunizations required a ⌐le.

*1
http://www
through: The
vaccine makes
the U.S. snuffed

nmunization schedule is found at
ee Carter, Richard, 1965, Break-
ut of favor for 20 years, the Salk
n, Jason, Wiping out polio: How

③ In the United States, the controversy ended after both men were dead. For many years, Sabin's oral vaccine was the only one administered in the U.S. Since 2000, however, the Salk vaccine has been the only one recommended by the Centers for Disease Control and Prevention (CDC) because of estimates that one person in about 2.4 million people in the U.S. contracts polio from the Sabin vaccine. But the Sabin vaccine is still considered preferable in areas around the world where polio occurs. One reason is that the live virus in the vaccine can spread immunity to people who haven't been vaccinated.

④ Both Salk and Sabin can be credited with the eradication of polio worldwide. In October 2012, fewer than 200 cases of polio had been reported.

Discussion Questions

1. *Argued* was used in the task to state a position. What other words or expressions were used to state or counter a position?

2. How is the controversy between Salk and Sabin set forth in this passage? What is the main organizational structure?

3. From what you now know about both vaccines, which would you argue for giving to children in the region or country where you were born?

4. Why do you think polio hasn't been totally eliminated?

5. Can you tell what the speaker's point of view is? Explain.

Task 4: Presentation of a Well-Known Figure

Choose one of these task options. Use suitable organizational structures, such as chronological order, comparison and contrast, and listing.

1. Biographical Sketch: Prepare a five-minute presentation in which you give a biographical sketch of a well-known person in your field or another related academic area. In deciding what information to include, consider what details about the person's early life may have formed the foundation for his or her later accomplishments.

2. Controversial Figure: Prepare a five-minute presentation on an influential but controversial figure and the impact of that person on your field of study. Provide biographical data about the person and then explain why he or she is controversial.

3. A Controversy: Prepare a five-minute presentation about a controversy between two well-known figures in your field or in another academic area. Give and discuss data that supports their positions. If you wish, include your own opinion.

Part 2: Presenting Research

Research presentations generally follow the same organizational pattern as research written for publication: Introduction, Methodology, Results, and Discussion. The purpose of the research is usually stated in the introduction.

Task 5: Writing Purpose Statements

Read the summary of a small study to determine what problems a group of non-native speakers of English had when writing purpose statements in research articles. Then, with a partner, answer the questions on page 175.

AN INVESTIGATION OF PURPOSE STATEMENTS WRITTEN
BY NATIVE SPEAKERS OF SPANISH

Non-native speakers of English who publish research articles in journals in their own language are sometimes asked to submit a summary or abstract of their research in English. These summaries usually include a one-sentence purpose statement that states the goal of the research. I was interested in finding out what specific problems non-native Spanish speakers had writing purpose statements in English.

In this study, I looked at a total of 60 purpose statements from four U.S. dental journals. Then I compared them to 60 purpose statements written in English by native speakers of Spanish in a Venezuelan dental journal.

In the U.S. dental journals, purpose statements had a relatively simple structure. The most common one was *The purpose of this study was to +* VERB. The next most common was *This study +* VERB.

The most common verbs that followed were *evaluate, compare, investigate,* and *determine* in that order—for example *the purpose of this study was to determine . . .* or *This study compared. . . .*

Most Common Structures in U.S. Dental Journals	Most Common Verbs in U.S. Dental Journals
The purpose of this study was to + VERB	*evaluate* *compare*
This study + VERB	*investigate* *determine*

Here are some differences I found. First, twice as many purpose statements—10 percent—were omitted all together in the Venezuelan dental journal. Only five percent were omitted in the American dental journals.

Purpose Statement Omitted	
American dental journals	5%
Venezuelan dental journals	10%

Second, instead of *in this study, the present study* was used about 22 percent of the time in the Venezuelan journal. It was only used once in the U.S. journals. *Present* is likely a translation from Spanish.

Use of *the Present Study* in place of *This*	
U.S. dental journals	1.7% (1 example)
Venezuelan dental journals	22%

Third, *work* was used in place of *study* in about 13 percent of the Venezuelan journals but not used at all in the American journals.

Use of *Work* in place of *Study*	
U.S. dental journals	0%
Venezuelan dental journals	13%

In several instances in the Venezuelan journal, both *work* or *investigation* and *study* occurred in the same purpose statement, as in *In the present work a study was done* . . . .

A fourth difference was that present perfect tense was used in several of the Venezuelan purpose statements but not in the U.S. purpose statements, which used past tense.

Use of Present Perfect Tense instead of Past	
U.S. dental journals	*The aim of this study was to compare* . . .
Venezuelan dental journals	*The aim of this study has been to compare* . . .

A fifth difference I found was that in the Venezuelan journal several purpose statements included the methodology that was used in the study rather than introducing the methodology in a separate sentence. There were no instances of this in the U.S. journals.

But the sixth and biggest difference I found was in how the writers viewed the goal of the purpose statement. In the U.S. journals, the purpose statement focused on the question the researcher intended to investigate. The assumption was that the answer would be found as the result of the study. But in the Venezuelan journal, more than 20 percent of the writers used the purpose statement to indicate the results of their study. So, for example, in one U.S. journal, the purpose statement

began with *The purpose of this study was to determine if . . .* ; but in

the Venezuelan journal, it was written as *In the present study we*

determined . . . .

Here are a few more examples.

Goal of the Purpose Statement	
U.S. Dental Journals	Venezuelan Dental Journal
The purpose of this study was to determine if...	*In the present study we determined...*
This paper investigates the factors that...	*This paper shows the factors that...*
The aim of this paper was to determine the effects....	*The aim of this paper was to prove the effects....*
The aim of this clinical study was to evaluate/assess	*The aim of the clinical study was to prove..*

The findings from this study of purpose statements should help

Spanish speakers who need to write purpose statements in English

as part of their research summary or abstract.

Discussion Questions

1. Label the sections: Introduction, Methodology, Results, and Discussion.

2. In the Methodology section, how is the information organized? How are the results organized?

3. Do you think the information is clearly displayed?

4. In the Discussion section, does the speaker use any hedging devices? (See Unit 5.)

5. In your opinion, what are weaknesses in the study? Do you think the speaker should have mentioned them?

6. Do you think the information in the presentation is useful for native speakers as well as non-native speakers?

The speaker summarizes the findings of a small research project. She first tells the audience why she did the study. Then, using chronological order, she briefly states how she carried out the study (Methodology). In the next section, she lists what she thinks are the interesting findings (Results), putting the most important one at the end. She's displayed the information using simple tables. For this study, they are adequate. She concludes by stating that non-native writers might benefit from these findings (Discussion). This study may be useful for any student who is writing research for the first time. One reason the study is limited is that it investigates purpose statements from only one group.

Summarizing the Methodology

Unit 3 focused on describing processes. If you are (1) reporting on research you conducted or (2) reporting on someone else's research, you will likely use chronological order in your Methodology (Methods and Materials) section to describe your procedure.

Task 6: Methodology Sections

Read the methodology sections. Then, working with a small group, answer the questions on page 177.

1. In this study, I began by looking at a total of 60 purpose statements from four U.S. dental journals. Then I compared them to 60 purpose statements written in English by native speakers of Spanish in a Venezuelan dental journal.

2. The study that Koeppe and Meisel carried out is a longitudinal study of simultaneous acquisition of German and French by thirteen pre-school children. They videotaped the children every two weeks for thirty minutes in each language, and then they transcribed both linguistic and non-linguistic interaction with their context.*

3. About ninety percent or eighty percent of the plantations in the central valley of Costa Rica were transformed to highly intensive coffee plantations. So, given this context, obviously one of the things that we started asking was what is the impact of this on biodiversity. So

we conducted [a study] just to find out what species we are definitely gonna lose because when you're eliminating those trees, you're eliminating the habitat for those species. So, we started with a very simple survey of trying to find out what's up there in the trees. And we use a methodology that is used commonly for studies of arthropods in the canopy of forest. Basically you fog the canopy of the tree with an insecticide unfortunately, and then the insects start dropping. You collect them, and then you quantify them.*

Discussion Questions

1. In the first excerpt, why did the speaker use *I*, as compared to *we* in the third excerpt?

2. In the second and third excerpts, where does each the Methodology section begin? What information precedes it?

3. List the connecting devices used by the speakers when they discuss the Methodology section of their research. How similar are each of these three excerpts?

4. Good speakers not only need to condense their research study in order to present it orally. They also need to be aware of their audience. Who is likely the audience in Excerpt 3? How can you tell? If the speaker were presenting a paper at a national conference on this topic, do you think you would understand it?

*From MICASE, with minor modifications.

Summarizing the Results

In the oral presentation on comparison of purpose statements in dental journals, the speaker displays the results in tables. Tables present information in columns and rows. In the presentation in Unit 5 on induction loops (see pages 133–35), the speaker presents information using a bar graph. Tables and graphs can enhance audience interest. And because they are visual representations of what the speaker is saying, they also help the audience follow the presentation In addition, they can be referred to during the question-and-answer period after the presentation.

Task 7

Look at the tables and graphs on this page and pages 179–80. Choose a table or graph to describe. Or choose the third and fourth graphs for a side-by-side comparison and contrast. What would you include in your introduction? Based on what the table or graph reveals, what results would you highlight? Would you point out or emphasize any unexpected results? Introduce and discuss the table and graph using expressions studied in Unit 5.

Average Expenditure per New Car (1967–2009)

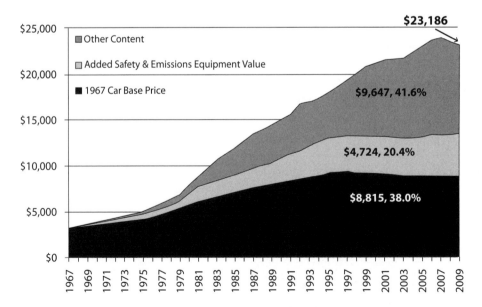

Source: Average Expenditure per New Car, *Wards' Automotive Yearbook 2010*, page 260.

Age Distribution of Social Networking Site Users in 2008 and 2010

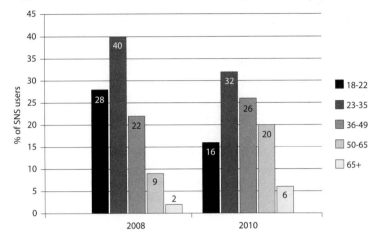

Source: Pew Research Center's Internet & American Life Social Network Site survey conducted on landline and cell phone between October 20–November 28, 2010.

Number of Children under Age 18 in the U.S.

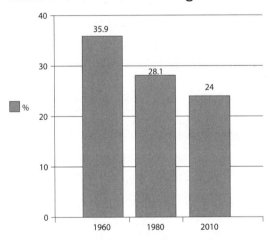

Source: U.S. Census Bureau.

Number of Adults over Age 65 in the U.S.

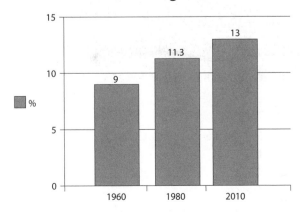

Source: U.S. Census Bureau.

U.S. Pet Statistics

U.S. households with a pet	62 percent
Number of dogs owned	Approximately 78.2 million
Number of cats owned	Approximately 86.4 million
Households with at least one dog	39 percent
Households with at least one cat	33 percent
Cost of owning a dog or cat	U.S.$600–900 per year

Source: Data from ASPCA, www.aspca.org/about-us/faq/pet-statistics.aspx and the Humane Society of the United States, www.humanesociety.org/issues/pet_overpopulation/facts/pet_ownership_statistics.html, compiled by American Pet Products Association.

Referring to Handouts

During your presentation, if you are passing out a handout to audience members, you will want to refer them to the handout or various pages on the handout as you speak. Here are some expressions used by speakers at a conference.*

❐ Several speakers use an *if* clause: *if you'll look, if you look*, to refer the audience to the handout.

❐ Notice how *you* is being used to instruct the audience: *now you look, so you turn the page.*

❐ Other expressions, such as *as shown, as it says, in table one, which shows* are frequently used when speakers are referring to tables and graphs.

1. *If you have a look at the handout they've just given you, the first results show*

2. *So you turn the page, table 3.*

3. *Take a look at table three. This is your page eight.*

4. *If you look at the second page of your handout,*

5. *In table one on page four of the handout, which shows . . . .*

*From *John Swales Conference Corpus* (2009). Ann Arbor: The Regents of the University of Michigan, with minor modifications.

6. *The numbers are given in table one on your handout.*

7. *Now as you can see in table two in your handout, . . .*

8. *Let's look at page two of your handout.*

9. *As it says in your handout, . . .*

10. *As shown in section two point two on page one of your handout . . . .*

11. *You've got some examples in the handout. I won't go into them in detail.*

12. *I've given the quotations from various books on your handouts.*

Task 8: Expressions that Refer to Handouts

Categorize each expression on page 180 and this page by its function.

1. Does it introduce the handouts?

2. Does it refer the audience to a specific page and/or table in the handout?

3. Does it refer to information in the handout that the speaker won't go into?

Discussion

Depending on the results of your study, in your Discussion section you may want to

- ❏ draw conclusions from your findings
- ❏ discuss implications of the study
- ❏ comment on the possible impact of the findings
- ❏ point out the limitations of the study
- ❏ discuss achievements of the study
- ❏ list questions raised by the study
- ❏ suggest future research

Preparing to Present Your Research

At one time or another, members of most academic fields face the prospect of presenting research findings to their colleagues or to a larger academic community. The requirements for giving research presentations may vary from one forum to another. Therefore, individual speakers first need to examine the particular context in which they will present their research. If you are presenting a research paper, you may want to consider these questions.

Physical Context	
Where will you present your talk?	
How many people can the room accommodate?	
What types of equipment will be in the room?	
Where will you stand?	

Academic Context	
What is the purpose of the forum?	
Have you seen others present in the same forum? If so, list some things that you've noticed about their presentations? (Or, have you been asked to use a particular format?)	
Who is your audience? What is your relationship to members of the audience? (Or, what do you want your relationship with the audience to be?)	
What are their expectations?	
How long will you have time to speak? Will there be time for questions?	

The academic context will in part determine what type of information you will include in your presentation. This, in turn, will determine what strategies you will choose to present the information. You now have a number of tools to depend on to make a good academic presentation.

Task 9: Choose Your Presentation

Give a six- to eight-minute oral presentation on one of these topics. Use the chart on page 184 to help you plan.

- a research study by someone in your field
- a research study you did as part of a group or on your own
- a experiment you conducted in a laboratory.
- a survey that you (and your group) conducted in your class

1. If you choose a topic that might be difficult for a general audience to understand, decide how you can present information so that so that the audience can follow you.

2. For your presentation, choose what connecting devices you will use to move from one section to another.

3. Decide what charts and graphs, if any, you will need to present your information.

4. Decide how you will conclude your presentation. Will you discuss one or more limitations, such as the sample size? Will you discuss the importance of the study? Further research?

5. If you are going to do a group presentation, decide what section of the research each of you will introduce.

Your Presentation	
What background information will you introduce?	
In your introduction, will you define a term (or terms)? Is a one-sentence definition enough or will you need to expand on your definition?	
Will you discuss prior research? If so, how will you organize the material (listing, chronologically, comparison and contrast, by categories/classification)?	
How will you introduce the topic of your research? How much detail will you give about how the topic emerged?	
How much detail will you give about your methodology?	
How will you organize information about the method you used to carry out your research? <ul><li>Will you list the characteristics of your subjects?</li><li>Will you discuss steps in a process (chronological order)?</li><li>Will you move from the most important aspects of your methodology to the least important?</li><li>Will you categorize information (subjects, documents, process, etc.)?</li><li>Will you give specific examples?</li><li>Will you include narrative about your subjects or your involvement in the process?</li></ul>	
How will you highlight results (listing, general to specific)?	
Will you use visuals? What kind?	
What will you emphasize in your Discussion section (a recommended solution to a problem, practical applications, evaluation of the research, a future possible study)?	
Will you prepare a handout for the audience? Will you include a bibliography?	

Task 10: Self-Evaluation

Write a self-evaluation that discusses the improvement you have made during the course. Include such topics as style, gestures, interaction with the audience, use of visuals or other devices, topic choice, organization and connecting words, and pace. Your instructor may want you to present this information to other class members so that they can add their comments.